Chagall

Chagall

Jean Cassou

Thames and Hudson
London

TRANSLATED FROM THE FRENCH BY ALISA JAFFA

Printed in Switzerland by Buchdruckerei Winterthur AG
and bound in Great Britain by
Cox & Wyman Ltd, London, Fakenham & Reading

Contents

Page   7   CHAPTER ONE
Chagall and his Childhood

21   CHAPTER TWO
Memories

55   CHAPTER THREE
Memories become Reality

77   CHAPTER FOUR
Russia

93   CHAPTER FIVE
Vocation

127   CHAPTER SIX
Chagall in France

169   CHAPTER SEVEN
Chagall and World Events

239   CHAPTER EIGHT
Chagall as a Religious Painter

267   Chronology

269   Short Bibliography

273   List of Illustrations

285   Index

Chagall and his Childhood

It is customary to explain the work of a creative artist – writer, poet or painter – by examining the course his life has taken, and to relate a study of his art and his style to his biography. There is a reason for this: his style, after all, develops over a period of time. Moreover, there are obvious links between this evolution and the artist's life which are worth illuminating. However, this biographical approach assumes a principle of determinism in the realm of the intellect which is liable to be exaggerated. This tendency is evident particularly in the opening chapter of all studies of this kind, in which the biographer traces the origins and early years of the artist under examination. In these beginnings the author will claim to discern the seeds of a development destined to follow an inevitable course, and in this way adopts the role of a prophet after the event. But of course such predictably infallible prophecies apply only to completely external, superficial circumstances such as social milieu, race, class or education, all of which are exemplified by features of his painting that are in themselves external and superficial, even exotic and picturesque.

The use of such an approach in a study of the work and character of an artist such as Chagall would merely arouse the impatience of Chagall himself. Obviously he is well aware of the fact that he is a Jew, a Russian Jew, born in Vitebsk in 1887 – he has said so himself any number of times, and it has been said about him and repeated even more often by others. He has told the story of his own childhood, and all kinds of scenes from his childhood appear very frequently in his works and are portrayed in a sufficiently distinctive and original manner for there to be no doubt as to what they are. However, this is not the place to discuss external features, or themes, motifs and subjects. In so doing we would merely remain on the surface of things, and would fail to discover the essential nature of a creative artist and of his art.

The study of this essential nature should really begin only at the moment when the man becomes the artist, that is, at the moment when he becomes aware of himself and of his art. The preceding period is prehistory, a prologue, a prelude. To see in it what in academic terms is known as sources is mere illusion. It never fails to annoy Chagall when people look to his personal origins for the sources of his art. Conscious of the range of his poetic talent, he balks at the necessity for such an approach. He points out that these origins, which have been dogmatically seized upon, in turn have origins of their own. The Hebrews, perhaps? But then there had been so much before the Hebrews, all the depths of an even more distant past. This is where he comes from, as do we all.

In this connection it is worth noting that we know a number of more or less mediocre artists who can be very adequately defined by this kind of study of origins. Indeed it is their origins that define them, that constitute their limitations. They are quite simply Jewish, German, Spanish or 'even' French artists, and have remained what they were at the moment their names were entered on a birth certificate long before they became aware of themselves, which is, as we have said, the only kind of birth that can interest us and that can produce a valid artist. But such mediocrities have never achieved this kind of birth. They are artists whose activities are strictly confined to national expression. They remain in their national milieu, in the limited world of their own origins, and behave as if from the first they had been astonished to find themselves there, delighted with the singular appearance of their environment, and as if they share our own delight at the discovery of its singularity. In our eyes this world, with its costumes, its customs, its setting, and its bric-à-brac, is a strange world. The mediocre artists, perhaps as a result of their natural limitations, and bent on using the given situation to its best advantage, themselves awake to its strangeness and throughout their careers think only of exploiting it.

1 *Woman with Basket*, 1906–7. Probably begun in Vitebsk while Chagall was still under Pen's tutelage, and completed in Saint Petersburg

2 *Peasant Woman*, 1907. This study, from a professional model, is in the typically academic style favoured by Chagall's instructors in Saint Petersburg

Now the true artist, who aspires towards universality and who seeks quite simply and honestly to be himself – and who consequently cares only for his art and not for the external appearances of his art, or for its motifs, themes and subjects – this artist, even if he were born and had spent his childhood in a 'foreign' milieu, would never consciously be aware of this. Chagall was never surprised at the singularity of what he saw around him; it is only to us that it appears singular. He was a part of his milieu and it obviously affected him, engendering certain sensations and emotions, but the idea never occurred to him that these sensations and emotions should have had anything special about them which needed only to be sufficiently emphasized to attract the curiosity of the countries to which he later happened to make his way. For it is in these lands that he was to be regarded as a stranger. It is our enchanted eyes that have made him a stranger. How dangerous for him! And how sad! To be no more than a stranger, a publicity agent of a foreign firm, a commercial traveller with foreign products – what kind of destiny is that? Can this have happened to him? But, happily, he is a true artist, a great artist. The surprise which the external aspect, the subjects of his art, aroused on his arrival in France displeased him; it is not the kind of surprise he aims to produce. Similarly, he has never believed that he was destined to become a stranger, even though as a child he lived in a world which to us may seem strange. For him it was simply the world of his childhood, his natural world. This was called a ghetto, a place which one cannot leave and which has become the symbol of all places from which escape is impossible. For him it was not *a* world, but *the* world, the cosmos.

Not until this has been taken into account may one speak of the importance of childhood impressions in the consciousness of an artist like Chagall. They are important not because they have supplied him with an array of themes, subjects and picturesque material, but because they were absorbed by an extremely keen and original sensibility. But let us leave aside the external source of these impressions so that we may remain in the field of pure subjectivity and consider

3 *The House in the Park*, 1908. Painted in Narva on the Baltic Sea, this belongs
to the modern style of the period, derived from Gauguin and Toulouse-Lautrec

how, in this sense, childhood impressions came to suffuse the imagery of a great painter.

These impressions were transformed into nostalgic memories of childhood. The soil upon which they fell was the fertile mind of a creative artist. This was no journalist instructed by his newspaper to investigate the land of childhood memories. Such a reporter, having donned the national costume of the country concerned and disguised himself as a child, would have taken notes, made sketches of isbas (pinewood chalets) with people inside them (and on top of them), of weddings and ceremonies, and would have then presented his public with his findings and would have proceeded with a further series of illustrations to please his readers' love of the exotic.

We must try to picture the mind of the creative artist, in which everything is a source of material, as the impressions of childhood undergo a metamorphosis and by a process of mental digestion, as it were, become assimilated for elaboration into paintings. This we may express as memories combined with nostalgia. This is not to say that a memory that is simply evoked, presents itself for passive contemplation. No, it involves a past that is dreamed of, longed for, and poignant, a past in action, a past endowed with a magic quality, a strange power of attraction. Time has secretly done its work. The impressions of childhood are reawakened and appear in a completely new guise, and the soul of the artist looks on in wonder. He assesses these impressions and questions them, sensing that they bear revelations and precious confidences. They appear to him to be charged with obscure and powerful energies, and he is eager to make use of them to enrich the equally mysterious composition he is in the course of evolving.

The theory behind these chronological studies is usually put in an abstract and schematic form which is clumsy in the extreme. It is preferable to adopt a completely different perspective and proceed not from the event to the created image, but from the image to the event. One must not recall the event until, transformed into a memory, it has appeared on canvas. Moreover, only those events should

13

4 *Self-portrait with Brushes*, 1909. This picture, reminiscent of the self-portraits of the Italian Mannerists and seventeenth-century Dutch painters, reveals self-assurance as well as a deliberate striving for effect

be recalled which have undergone this process. Such a method might appear to be absurd, but it is nevertheless appropriate to the procedures involved in matters of the mind. When all is said and done, an artist's entire *œuvre* and at the same time his person, his existence, in short all that is implicit in the mention of his name, is a complete entity, an organic whole, a universe. For the purposes of an investigation of this universe, one can single out different elements and point out certain trends. But it is important never to lose sight of the living personality at the centre of this universe, his unpredictable movements, or his very existence.

There is a saying of Nietzsche's that I found in the ninth fragment of the *Fröhliche Wissenschaft* (*Joyful Wisdom*), entitled 'Our Eruptions', which strikes me as appropriate here: 'The son often reveals the father to himself; for the latter understands himself better since he has had a son.' In every previous existence there are concealed, unrecognized forces that do not erupt until much later. In the same way past incidents reappear in his work in a form that is brimming with real life, taking on a reality of their own. Now it is this reality alone that interests us, for it is a part of life and not a matter of chronology. The result of this vital eruption is that the incident from the past assumes a place and a shape. It exists. By contrast, all the host of far more lively incidents, which at one time accompanied this one and hid it from view, no longer exist – they have fallen into oblivion.

More often than not chronology is nothing more than the unearthing of a whole succession of forgotten events. But one such event has remained on the edge of the abyss – this one no longer belongs to the past, it has taken on reality, it has found its way into the present: it has become a memory.

One does not have to be particularly old to experience the return of those childhood memories that have not disappeared into oblivion. For the most part, no doubt, it is the old who delight in describing their memories. But theirs is a totally different kind of indulgence,

5 *Portrait of my Fiancée in Black Gloves*, 1909. Chagall's first portrait of Bella, and an early masterpiece

6 *The Holy Family*, 1909. Painted in Vitebsk during one of Chagall's frequent visits from Saint Petersburg

it is calculated and deliberate. The reawakening that I have in mind, this resurgence of childhood impressions, this revival of impressions that have become memories, is not consciously controlled. They appear to the creative artist in a demanding and peremptory manner at that unforeseen moment of inspiration, and so produce a work of art. Quite often this metamorphosis may even occur quite close to childhood, when a man has only just bid his childhood farewell. He is at the point of leaving it behind, he has just emerged from

17

his childhood and is missing it when impressions surge up within him, and already they are memories.

This phenomenon is even more marked if the man is able to preserve the greater part of his childhood within himself for as long as possible. This is the case with Chagall. In people like him there is an inborn identification with the condition of childhood, as if this were their homeland. And in their earliest emotions they have perceived the disturbing communication to which they will have access when these emotions return in the form of memories. For them childhood is a stream in which they delight to feel submerged. They have had a special relationship to their childhood and this will always remain. Such is the gift of childhood – for those who have been granted it their childhood impressions will be more vivid than those of others.

7 *The Dead Man*, painted in 1908 when Chagall was twenty-one years old

8 *Birth*, 1910. One of a series of narrative compositions painted during Chagall's last months in Saint Petersburg, this work counterposes two scenes: the female, dominated by the colour red, and the male in which yellow predominates

Then, too, the transformation of these impressions into memories will occur in a far more dramatic form than with other people. In a word, they always remain involved with their childhood, and it is in terms of their childhood that their existence unfolds and their genius develops. They are aware that it is a thing to preserve and prolong, a salvation to grasp.

Thus, one of the fears experienced by Chagall in the course of his childhood – and there were many – was concerned with passing from childhood to adolescence. 'I was afraid of my imminent coming of age ...', he records in *My Life*. And further on he says: 'Once I had turned thirteen, my carefree life would come to an end and all my sins would fall upon my head.' He would then be unprotected,

19

and this was enough to instill real terror. Whence this desperate need to keep within reach of the tears of innocence, to watch over the tiny magic flame of his heart, to be perpetually on the watch for the bountiful treasury of memories? A little later, at the time of his first works, that is at the time he took up the life of an artist, suddenly these memories began to appear. His famous, early masterpiece *The Dead Man* (*Ill. 7*), which is a lyrical and haunted résumé of his entire childhood, is dated 1908, when he was twenty-one years old. It was in 1921, when he was thirty-four, that he began to write *My Life*. This would seem rather young to be writing one's memoirs, but it was not meant as a definitive, retrospective assessment – an old man's hobby, as we have already said – but a record of that constant relationship with his childhood which has persisted throughout his whole life. For at the time when he was seized by the need to tell the story of his life, or that part of his life which had only just begun to slip past, he returned to his native Russia. There once again he encountered his childhood and tried desperately to recapture it and perpetuate it.

This attempt was all the more urgent since events had taken place that were threatening reality itself, the reality of objects and of places whose soul he was hoping to rediscover. He often tells how on his return to Russia he had a strong feeling that everything he had known was about to disappear and that it was essential to record it all with the utmost speed, to preserve its imprints and its tradition. What probably happened was that, like all those who return to the scenes of their past, he no longer recognized them as being exactly as he had left them. However, apart from this the country was in the grip of war, and was about to be subjected to one of the most overwhelming upheavals in the history of the world – namely, the October Revolution. This was enough to dispel all memories. Nothing would ever be the same as before. Hence the desperate necessity to record all that could still be recorded.

CHAPTER TWO

Memories

The Dead Man, as I have mentioned, was painted in 1908. It was produced in Saint Petersburg, where Chagall had been living for a year. His mother had yielded to the child's desire to become a painter – a strange desire, which could hardly have been induced by anything in his home environment. But his mother was a kindly woman with an alert and positive mind, and after her initial reaction of utter dismay she resigned herself to the situation. His uncle Pissanewsky, an enlightened man with a number of contacts in the outside world, who had even heard of the fame of Repin, supported him in his decision. So the child was placed in the school of Pen, a Jewish artist in Vitebsk, who painted genre pieces and portraits. Later the young Marc was sent to continue his studies in Saint Petersburg. Thus there is a certain distance, both in time and space, separating the extraordinary picture of *The Dead Man* (*Ill. 7*) from the childhood recollections to which it belongs. For this is indeed a memory, an early, strange and haunting memory.

Others were to appear in the same manner, memories of important events – funerals, weddings, births, all of which impressed themselves on the mind of the child. Later in Paris, in an atmosphere remote from these simple and religious events, right from the start Chagall's art was dominated by memories. It was as if they had to be and always would be the essential core of his art. Even more so, as this vast world in which the young apprentice had immersed himself was so different from his native microcosm. He was sublimely happy there in his own niche, absorbing all these profound impressions. In Saint Petersburg he had been made to feel different, to feel his *strangeness*, to remember that he was a Jew; he had had to obtain papers and authorizations, to observe formalities. In short, he had always had something to fear and could never feel at ease. These appalling hindrances disappeared in Paris, and he now began to live life to the full. Yet the difference still persisted. It was no longer a painful one, but none the less evident for all that. For in Paris this extraordinary feeling of emancipation together with the discovery of modern painting and painters, the discovery of a high level of civilization, and on the other hand the poverty, the bohemian existence, the struggle and the novelty of all this served only to heighten the insistent onslaught of memories.

The memories demand absolute power, and they receive it. The field is wide open to them. In the guise of nostalgia they use this effective weapon together with all their creative virtues, and giving themselves free reign they create a legend. A legend which will become what today we must acknowledge as the universe of Chagall. Obviously this universe has been enriched by all kinds of subsequent developments. But from the moment of its inception it was complete and as it was always to remain.

It is not surprising that those first pictures of Chagall's universe should have been masterpieces. If a legend is to take root it can only do so by means of masterpieces. There must be immediacy and the splendour and totality of revelation. And this applies to the astounding series of works assembled in the year 1911. This revelation in *Russian Village, from the Moon* (*Ill. 10*) is brimming with lyricism, and in *Dedicated to my Fiancée* (*Ill. 9*) or in *The Holy Carter* (*Ill. 11*) it is tinged with an astonishing feeling of burlesque. One feels that this carter must have been in a very playful mood to have adopted the shape of a flying pipe. And one wonders what demon could have possessed Cendrars – for it was he who provided Chagall with his titles at that time – when he gave his friend the idea of dedicating to his fiancée this figure in a red dressing gown with a bull's head, taken from heaven knows what primitive cult or malicious village custom. But he was probably right: this whole ironical jumble corresponds to things from a very remote past, which still command a wealth of

9 (*right*) *Dedicated to my Fiancée*, 1911. This is one of the first major works of Chagall's Paris first period, and one of the few that he completed on one occasion (in a single night)

10 (*left*) *Russian Village, from the Moon*, 1911. The vivid atmosphere of unreality here is due as much to the plastic motifs as to the interplay of geometrical forms

tenderness and which could not hope for worthier celebration than to be offered this day in homage to the beloved. But *I and the Village* (*Ill. 12*) and *To Russia, Asses, and Others* (*Ill. 15*) in particular still remain the principle works of this culminating period in Chagall's imagination. These two poetic works are as insistent as they are complex. At this moment of transplantation the most intimate aspects of the poet's life are evoked by the onrush of memories which by their own momentum assemble themselves and suggest their own representation.

Like every legend, this one, too, has its ritual words and its sacred animals, its magic objects and its fetishes that recur prophetically. But Chagall rejects the symbolic character that has been attributed

24

11 *The Holy Carter*, 1911. The importance of the circular arrangement of the composition is shown by the fact that the picture was originally hung the other way up, representing a man seated. It was first hung this way up by Herwarth Walden at the Berlin exhibition in 1914

to these objects. He distrusts the word *symbolism* as much as the word *literature*. He never stops repeating that all he wants is to paint. His outspoken declaration to James Johnson Sweeney has often been quoted: 'If you ask Chagall to explain his paintings, even today he will still reply: "I don't understand them at all. They are not literature. They are merely a pictorial arrangement of images that obsess me..."' Let us abide by this formula, which is the clearest definition of the only creative mechanism that Chagall would admit to. For our part we shall leave it at that. These objects that obsess him are memories, which is quite enough to confer upon them an extraordinary strength without making us feel obliged to recognize in them representations of some more profound motivation. They are valid in themselves, they have their own definite significance. They are possessed of their own charm, and it is such that it exercises a fascinating and obsessive power.

Flowers, isbas, oil lamps, samovars, carts, cows and the beautiful, tender eyes of cows, candlesticks and the flickering light of candles, violins and fiddlers, snatches of music overheard, odours inhaled, all the minor gods that haunted the child – who can deny their power, since these themes have repeatedly returned and asserted themselves in the genius of the painter? The small town of Vitebsk, the course of its provincial days, its familiar figures, the Jewish customs, the Jewish festivals, none of these mean anything, they are simply statements without any further additions or suppositions, and the mere fact that they should have existed is reason enough for them to reappear, to remain, and it is this way in which they remain, this persistence, which is important for it is an element in the creative mechanism of a great poet.

It is nevertheless legitimate to look for a direction in this mechanism and possibly even for symbols. An isba might never have aroused any memories were it not for the fact that it is indissolubly linked – to the point of provoking tears of affection or anguish – with those blue houses of his childhood. It is understandable that Chagall refuses to examine his own subconscious. A painter paints,

12 *I and the Village*, 1911. This painting, in which the composition is again based on diagonals and circular forms, represents both the terminal point and the peak of Chagall's 'geometrical' series

and he cannot regard his painting as a symbol of anything. He is right. But the psycho-analysts are not wrong if, within their own limits, they regard the work of Chagall as the most fertile territory for exploration.

One example alone is enough to demonstrate that it is impossible to study Chagall without making use of their interpretations. To this end I have selected the interpretation of *To Russia, Asses and Others* (*Ill. 15*) which appears in an American study (Daniel E. Schneider, *A Psychoanalytic Approach to the Painting of Marc Chagall*. College Art Journal, New York, Vol. VI, No. 2, Winter 1946). This painting is certainly one of the most enigmatic of all Chagall's works. The oddity and incoherence are absolutely unfathomable in this

13 (*left*) *The Sleigh*, 1911. One of Chagall's Russian motifs in painterly style

14 (*above*) *Full Moon*, 1911. Like *To Russia, Asses and Others* (*Ill. 15*), this is one of the 1911 nocturnal scenes

painting, with the green monkey and green lamb being suckled by a reddish cow on a yellow roof, near the dome of a church, while through the vast black sky a woman holding a green bucket in her hand is descending, her head severed. The head is drifting to one side, the eye starting out of its socket, the mouth wide open, apparently more surprised at its surroundings than we are ourselves. The following is an explanation of this mystery that might have emerged had the artist been analysed by our eminent American doctor (the reference to his grandfather refers to an occasion when, after being missing all day, he was finally found perched on the roof of the house, gorging himself on carrots):

This is the place where I should like to be, sucking at the breast – just as my grandfather escaped on to the roof one day, I should like to escape from everyone who is trying to separate me from the breast and the body of Mother Earth. I am a little lamb, with the gift of imagination.

But perhaps I must resign myself to being weaned after all, for that old witch, the Dry Nurse, is quite capable of pursuing me for all my attempts to cling to my beloved teats.

This is equivalent to castration – to snatch me from the body of the one I love, I and the other little lambs, too, that are led to the slaughterhouse.

If I caught my witch, I would tear out her mouth and her eyes, and reduce her body to nothing but a breast. I would cut off the head of this beastly servant of civilization and the church, both of whom instituted this ridiculous idea of weaning us, and who have similarly upheld the authority of my parents and grandparents.

When I put this explanation to Chagall, as we stood in front of this canvas in the Musée National d'Art Moderne in Paris, he looked at me in bewilderment. Yet it is undeniable that many of the preoccupations uncovered and scientifically documented by psychoanalysis figure in his work – the subject of weaning, for example, which corresponds to castration, not to mention flight, an essential theme in the imagery of Chagall, and which is accepted as a symbol of the desire for the sexual act. But it is common for an artist to have no knowledge of such matters, and to him they belong in the pages

15 *To Russia, Asses and Others*, 1911

16 *The Birth,*
1911

of a text-book which he feels bound to leave unopened. Such works
are only for our use.

Nevertheless, however valuable we might find this text-book,
however enlightening, useful and convenient its information, we
will not linger over it. For we wish to approach the subject with a
fresh mind. Our subject is impervious to analysis because he is an
artist and is quite convinced that all he will find in our text-book
are everyday words, his own words and ours – words such as love,

17 (*right*) *Madonna with Child*, also of 1911

Chagall 1911

18 *The Soldier*, 1911

death and time – which if they present a problem do so in a common and universal fashion. This is what it always amounts to, and the artist knows that this is what he is saying, even if he is not aware of doing so. His role is to record memories. These may take the form of fantasies to which he does not have the key. And when others, whose profession it is, hand him the key he is somewhat taken aback. However, once he has overcome his surprise, what is the significance of it all for him? It contains exactly what he put into it – his memories. He recorded them without looking any further. Indeed, had he looked further this would have been dangerous.

Thus his childhood impressions were unusually intense and profound. I and the village – yes, there had been this passionate relationship between him and this village, there had been the smell of herrings and the taste of gherkins, the prayers in the synagogue, and not

19 *(right) Man with Scythe*, 1911

20 *The Mirror*, 1911–2, a nude from Chagall's Fauvist phase

21 *The Wedding*, 1911

only these things and all that has been attributed to the exclusive influence of Judaism, but the stable and the hen-house provided just as much excitement and as many wonderful impressions. And finally, nature itself, that has no specific religious colouring, nature, with its days and nights, its suns and moons, its blossoms and its snows, was welcomed by the mind of this child who was to be saturated with it forever in a way that even the greatest poets have never been. Once the mind of this child had become the mind of the artist these impressions immediately returned in the form of memories, arousing a heart-rending nostalgia. What was this? The urgent need to retain them. How? Well, since we are dealing with the mind of an artist, obviously in the form of images.

These images are open to symbolic interpretation. But one can just as easily dispense with the interpretations, or possibly keep them in reserve rather like the text-book we have mentioned for occasional consultation. It is not the works of reference that hold the essential clue, but the images themselves and the way in which they are assembled and composed. And I have already said that they are composed like a legend. Now this is the quality that poets, or at least the most gifted poets, have; perhaps this is the most distinctive aspect of their work, that from their memories they create a legend, a mythology, a fable, a fairy tale. Such a tale can be translated into psycho-analytical terms or it can quite simply be told as a story. The narrator has no other aim than to tell his tale. This is enough for him. He has put much into it, including elements that come from deep inside him, which he himself does not recognize.

But, while memories are composed in the telling and are deployed to form a sort of comedy or drama, we do not know all that they contain, the full weight of their significance. And the narrator himself is unaware of it, the more so because memories actually experienced are intermingled with memories of dreams, and from the outset the child made no distinction between his real impressions and his fantasies and dreams. When one reads *My Life*, Chagall's admirable book of early impressions, one is struck by its fairy-tale character. There is a fairy-tale tone, a distinctive note in the delivery and, beneath this delivery, humorous or kindly implications like silent smiles. Chagall possesses the gift of this style, and it is a great gift. It is remarkable that Bella too should have possessed this same gift. She used this same fairy-tale style in her memoirs, another fine book entitled *Lamps Lit*, which she felt compelled to write in her mother tongue. In it Bella relates her childhood, all that took place before *The First Meeting* (which was to be the subject of another book). Thus husband and wife offered each other that part of their lives that took place before they met as a way of completing their subsequent holy and fruitful union. They met like two creatures of the same species, favoured by the same gift and the same precious

knowledge that their childhoods, later consecrated by destiny, would continue and would re-echo throughout their whole existence. Moreover, they have the faculty of describing their childhoods in a discreet and dream-like fashion, in a particular style, the style of a fairy tale.

This is the style that governs Chagall's book, lending the objects and people in it an indescribably lost and mythical air. It is a jumble of recent and distant events, passing from one moment to another, from one set of circumstances to another. There is no attempt to restrict events to the setting in which they occurred, instead they are rediscovered in the separate, distinct and purely spiritual area that constitutes the memory, and memory is the story-teller. This is to say it assembles its memories in an order peculiar to itself, in un-expected sequences, it evokes them, and plays an active, inventive and creative role.

Therefore the pictorial images, which are the final transformation of the impressions derived from the original reality, and are their plastic representation, appear on the canvas in complete disregard of the rules of composition. The things that take place, or allegedly take place, do so regardless of time or place, everywhere and nowhere, in some corner where there happens to be room, and at whatever time the capricious memory has chosen. One character enters and then another, and there is no connection between them in space, and no proportion, just as there is no logical link between one episode and another. But are we entitled to raise any objections to memory, to make the slightest attempt to call it to order?

It is a teller of tales. In this it is like a people with no history, or with no further history. The Jews are indeed a historic people, and their history is written down in the Bible in the form of glorious chronicles, with each historic character and each story or event in its place, interspersed with the enumeration of individuals, the gen-ealogies, references to places, and the computation of years. But all this was long ago, and the Bible has become the book of books, that is to say not a book that one keeps on account of the great deeds

23 (left) Nude with Raised Arm, 1911

24 *Composition*, 1912

it contains, or to consult occasionally for its vast store of knowledge. It is the book that one reads. And one reads it because it tells stories, stories that are terrible and moving, stories that are arresting and interesting, moral stories, edifying stories, instructive stories and encouraging stories, all of which are company on the road of life for every human being aspiring to piety and wisdom. It is, in the strongest sense of the word, a popular book.

Immediately one uses this adjective and refers to the popular soul, popular art, popular songs and folklore, one is referring to something that is not historic, something outside history, that comes within the province of the story and the fable. When they ceased to be an historic nation all that was left to the Jews in their small communities throughout the Diaspora was to recall the lofty deeds – or abominations – of their kings, like so many fables, and indeed many of them became story-tellers like Peretz and Shalom Aleichem.

Chagall's painting has the character of the fable, it belongs to this enchanted kingdom. It is a fable and a collection of fables. *The Dead Man (Ill. 7)*, *I and the Village (Ill. 12)*, *To Russia, Asses and Others (Ill. 15)* – these early works are fables, and in them memories intermingle as they do in the book in which Chagall described them, without any particular attempt to keep to a sequence of time or a strict definition of place. Instead he uses obsessionally recurring objects and beings like magic incantations or litanies in the manner of folk tales. Separate events have fused into one image. Definition no longer matters. Only the impression remains, and vividly embodied in the memory it subsequently takes shape in the image. The exact description of events has been left behind and has evolved into the stuff of folk tales and poetry, with its formula, *once upon a time…* But which time? When? And where?

A woman rushes out into the street, arms outstretched and wailing with grief. Such scenes were commonplace enough in the ghetto, and yet they never failed to cause tumult and disorder, and were inevitably accompanied by displays of unrestrained pathos. But the first time a child is exposed to such sudden uproar, especially when

25 *The Cattle Dealer*, 1912. The relationship of beast to man emerges with extraordinary rhythm and vitality in this Cubist painting

the cause is death, it is a profound shock. At another time – although it was to become the same time, the *once upon a time* of fairy tales – there was the incident of the grandfather who had disappeared on the day of a festival. No one could think what might have happened to him. They began searching for him and calling him. In the end he was discovered perched on the roof, feasting on carrots. This was the maternal grandfather, the butcher who lived in Lyozno, a village fifty miles from Vitebsk on the road to Smolensk, where young Marc often used to go and breathe all the odours of country life, where he used to watch the animals being slaughtered. He also used to see his uncle Neuch there and would accompany him when he went to the peasants to buy their cattle. This was the uncle who played the fiddle ('he used to play like a shoemaker'). It is he, not

the grandfather, whom we see on the roof, not eating carrots but scraping away at his fiddle. The roof is that of the shoemaker with its sign, a boot hanging on the end of a rod, standing out grotesquely against the lurid yellow sky. Sweeney has shown how these are different memories that have merged and been telescoped together. Lionello Venturi and Franz Meyer have examined them with equal care.

The painting also shows a road-sweeper and a man disappearing either between two houses or into one of them – whichever it is, his dismay is expressed by the flowerpots he has let fall to the ground. Then, of course, there is the chief figure, lying with face uncovered on the bare earth street and surrounded by six burning candles. Thus a whole group of unrelated subjects appear integrated in the tale of

The Dead Man, also often known as *Candles in the Dark Street*. But this concentration of conflicting elements into one single dramatic scene, into one story, contributes to the story-like character of the painting and constitutes its nature and soul, placing it outside time and space, and taking us with it into a sphere of unreality in which we hear disturbing echoes. They are all the more disturbing, all the more serious and important for us, since, it must be emphasized, this is Chagall's first communication, his first truly characteristic work, his Minerva issuing out of his head fully armed with all his marvels and powers of sorcery, complete, unchallengeable, the very incarnation of his genius. Here, too, psycho-analysis has its part to play. It can trace the connections between these absurd images and can relate them to one central idea, the terror aroused in the conscious and unconscious mind of a child by its first encounter with death. But such considerations remain feeble and abstract when confronted with the processes of the creative genius, whereby profound and extremely varied childhood impressions are brought into juxtaposition with terrifying and distressing nocturnal accounts murmured in hushed tones of alarm and despair.

Psycho-analysis can also reveal the significance of flight, an immensely insistent theme in the work of Chagall. But the important thing for us is to grasp all that may have been in the soul of Chagall as a child, to share in the experience of the desire to fly. The intensity of this experience confirms the process we have outlined, whereby early impressions coalesced to produce this miracle which is the fable. For the fable is not subject to the limitations of time and place; it is, as it were, suspended in air. This, according to his memoirs, is the outcome of the predisposition Chagall had as a child for plunging perspectives, his love of the view from some high window looking out into the far distance, above the rooftops, on a level with the birds and the stars.

Apart from this there was his mania, which he shared with the rest of his family, for climbing up on the roof. What a temptation on a fine day, just like the day – a festival, no less – when his grand-

26 *The Fiddler*, 1912–3. The vigorous movement that pervades this work heralds the dynamic style of the figure studies and *genre* pictures that were to follow

27 *Peasant Eating*

father, the butcher, had settled himself up there with his carrots! This was also the best vantage point from which to watch fires, of which there were many in the wood-built town, and they provided magnificent spectacles. 'My sad and joyful town! As a boy, I used to look out on you from the doorstep of my childhood days. You seemed so bright to the eyes of a child. When the wall blocked my view, I used to climb up on a small boundary post. And if I still couldn't see, then I would climb right up on the roof. Why not? My grandfather used to go up there, too. And then I could look out over you at my ease.' Elsewhere he writes: 'I could see everything in great detail from the little window in our attic. I used to kneel down and put my head outside, and breathe in the cool, blue

28 (*right*) *My Parents*, 1912–3

29 *Still Life*, 1912

air. The birds would fly past right in front of me.' For him the obsession with flight is not merely a mask for the desire, common to
all children, to know what to make of the sexual act and ultimately
to perform it oneself; in him it was just as much an upsurge of his
whole physical being, expressing itself in imaginary visions, dreams
or attitudes. In short, it constituted an experience. Man has the desire
to fly, according to psycho-analysis. But here is an instance of this
desire taking a quite extraordinary hold, right through childhood,
and then recurring in all the pictures which the artist has painted
during his adult life. Surely here is an exception to the general rule,
a special case that belongs only to the field of art, which specializes
in exceptions.

The severed heads are similarly part of a symbolic language. As a child, Chagall's imagination was crammed with all manner of weird fantasies and there are numerous examples of these. He would cry when he heard the *badchan* singing and shouting, 'Bride, bride, stop and think who awaits you!' 'At these words', he tells us, 'my head would gently leave my body to go off and cry somewhere near the kitchens where the fish was being prepared.' There is another memory in which it is night, and as he falls asleep the child hears his uncle

30 *Calvary*, 1912. The starting point of this monumental representation of the Crucifixion was one of Chagall's Russian drawings, and it was first exhibited by Walden in Berlin under the title *Dedicated to Christ*

31 *Orpheus*, 1912. This was painted, says Chagall, 'to test myself against tradition and renew a connection with it'

Neuch playing the rabbi's song on his fiddle. 'My head flies lightly round the room on its own.' It is clear that during all his childhood he was moving towards this phantasmagorical world that he was to create and make his own. With all his flesh and blood he was destined to be free, and already felt himself to be free of the bonds of gravity: disorientated, dislocated, disjointed, on the threshold of levitation, on the point of no longer being attached to the earth and restricted by its laws, of no longer being static, situated in one particular place, but on the point of escaping from all this, of forgetting himself and melting away into an unattainable infinity.

Although this is outside the scope of psycho-analytical reference works, we may perceive within the vivid universe of Chagall the

32 *The Lovers*, 1913–4

prominence given to the association between flight and music. We do not need a psycho-analytical dictionary to tell us that the word for this equation is love. All these impressions that affected the child to the point of obsession result in the delightful images of flight and music which are fundamental to his work, and which are forever being brought together in images of love. For what these three elements of flight, music and love have in common is that they are free, for they can only flourish in freedom and they are made for infinity. They create ecstasy, they are ecstasy, that is to say they are the projection beyond the self, outside the ordinary condition of men enslaved by the co-ordinates of time and space. Lovers will be borne aloft above the town, lovers will hide their joy in the foliage of the highest trees. Fishes, like the birds, inhabit a region without contours or delineations, without height or depth, where they compete with each other in their aerobatic skill. And everywhere these aerial feats are accompanied by music, for music too is everywhere. The fiddler plays on his own body, which has become a 'cello (*Ill. 104*). Clocks, in their turn, will fly away and join the dance (*Ill. 123*). For a vast, undefined, undefinable space can be changed only into time, and time itself is by definition 'a river without banks'.

It appears that Bella borrowed the title for this famous painting from a text by Mallarmé. Chagall does not find his own titles. We know that at one time most of them were suggested by Cendrars. This is understandable: he is afraid to give his creation a name. A title, the definitive and irrevocable description given by a name, is a serious thing. This is in the domain of literature, of symbolism. Let the painter keep his silence. For our part, however, there is nothing to keep us from looking beneath the surface and surveying the exceptional and vital success with which he has assembled his memories, desires, dreams and all the faces of his people and turned them into this truly eloquent imagery of love.

33 *Woman*

CHAPTER THREE

Memories become Reality

In 1912–13, during his first stay in Paris, up to the time of his departure for Berlin, Chagall was translating his memories on to canvas in an ever more direct, naked and straightforward manner. The poetic process whereby some childhood impression becomes a memory in order to play its part in some enigmatic fable is no longer in evidence. What strikes us immediately about these pictures is their objective portrayal, without any hint of the mysterious in them. They are true to life, deriving from Marc Chagall's own place of origin, and are in marked contrast to the intoxicating medley of varied and unusual works being produced around him by other pilgrims from all over the world who had gathered in Montparnasse and Montmartre. Chagall now painted Jews at prayer, rabbis, men and women carrying water, rustic scenes, fiddlers, wooden houses in the snow or by moonlight. Almost the only one that is still somewhat fantastic is *Burning House* (*Ill. 39*), no doubt because this surprising and pathetic kind of spectacle affected the deepest areas of his unconscious as a child. But none of the other paintings arise from these areas of experience. They are no more than the straightforward testimonies of memory, a memory that attempts no transfiguration and only fulfils its ordinary function. La Ruche, where Chagall was living, was near the Vaugirard slaughter-houses, and these immediately recalled the memory of the scenes in his grandfather's butcher's shop, so the artist quite naturally began to work on this theme. These statements of memory, this homage to the unadorned sovereignty of memory, are taken up again in the two allegorical figures of a tall pregnant woman with her womb open like a window revealing the child within, *Russia* and *Pregnant Woman* (*Ill. 37*). The obvious, explicit

34 *Self-portrait in Front of House*, 1914. Painted in Vitebsk, this shows the self-confi-
dent and smartly dressed young painter standing in front of his parents' house

35 *Over Vitebsk*, 1914. Here is Vitebsk as seen from the room in which Chagall painted many of his 1914 canvases, showing the Ilytch church on the right

meaning of these two paintings is: I was born, says the artist, in one particular country and I bring you the message of my homeland.

After his short stay in Berlin, during which he saw his works illuminate the walls of the *Sturm* gallery, Chagall found himself once more in his homeland. He returned to the source of his memories, to his origins. He covered this distance in order to re-live the time to which his memories belonged. This Russian-Jewish milieu, these surroundings, these conditions of race, family and religion: it would have been inappropriate for me to introduce these factors until they actually became relevant to the scene and played their part in the guise of memories and nostalgia. It now becomes necessary to recall them a second time, because this time they appear in reality. Chagall,

57

36 *Paris through the Window*, 1913. The major work of Chagall's first Paris period, in which he 'commemorates the sensuous-spiritual experience of the city' (Franz Meyer)

now a fully-grown adult, went in search of this reality in order to see it once more, to verify it and thus to end his separation from it, a separation that had proved most fertile and productive. He rushed to confront the scene that was familiar and at the same time new to him – familiar because it represented his past and the past of others older than he, new because for him it was a rediscovery, and redis-

37 *(right) Pregnant Woman*, 1912–3. The idea for this picture probably originated with the *Maria Blacherniotissa*, the Byzantine Madonna type

39 *Burning House*, 1913. Like the *Pregnant Woman* (*Ill.* 37), this canvas is painted primarily in yellows and blazing reds

covery is always part discovery. To discover something, no matter how familiar it may appear, is to see it afresh as if for the first time. Certain things exist, but it is not enough to say they exist because they have already existed for some time. They are there; and this presence in itself represents an amazing force. These things are real, and yet it is necessary to convince oneself of their reality and to say so with the utmost assurance. And this assurance, too, is tinged with surprise, a surprise that borders on admiration and wonder.

38 (*left*) *Self-portrait at the Easel*, 1914. Another of the many self-portraits Chagall painted in Vitebsk in 1914

Thus, in the works inspired by Chagall's return and by his re-discoveries, we note the phenomenon already observed in the works composed towards the end of his time in Paris: gone are the spells and charms, the travelling magician has returned home, he is at ease in his own surroundings once again. He applied himself eagerly to his work, painting ceaselessly and drawing with strength and vitality (this is a period rich in black-and-white works). In short, his major preoccupation at this time was to produce what he calls *documents*.

In this he was spurred on by the great contemporary upheavals that were taking place. The whole past that he had just rediscovered and that had seemed likely to continue indefinitely now seemed in danger of changing, indeed of disappearing altogether. It was essential to have documents recording all this reality, for this was reality, which is a stupendous thing, and one which might well be in a precarious condition.

For the moment, then, the driving force within the artist upon his return to his native Vitebsk was this urgent need to recognize everything, to note everything, to put it on record, and thus to satisfy his emotions and gather together a harvest of documents. These documents consisted of familiar domestic and family scenes. There was nothing and no one that did not evoke a response in him. He even went in search of his former teacher, Pen, and on certain days during the year 1917 the two of them would go off together and work on the same motif, in Vitebsk and in the surrounding countryside overlooking the town where it was possible to see and take in the whole of Vitebsk (*Ill. 44*). He experienced feelings of homely and pleasurable intimacy with all that he encountered and saw afresh in this way. It was the intimacy in particular that the critic Abraham Efross praised in the twenty-five canvases that Chagall had contributed to the exhibition, 'The Year 1915', at the Michailova Art Salon in Moscow. The prodigal son was very favourably received by the Russian art world, which despite the war was very much alive. Tugendhold and Efross, both important art critics, very soon proved to be understanding and helpful friends. What had been memories

40 *Jew In Green*, 1914

41 *The Praying Jew*, 1914. The only one of the 'old Jew' pictures with a religious
theme

were now immediate realities, and the young Russian painter who had returned to his native land felt himself in complete harmony with these realities. He had achieved that harmony known as realism. This is a term that gives rise to endless discussions. However, it is quite clear when applied to an artist who has the same harmonious relationship with the world around him that he has with himself. It is, in short, an art based upon an inner and outer state of equilibrium. I am perfectly aware that Chagall claims to detest realism, and we shall return to this issue, which is a fundamental one. But it seems to me that this term may be applied to the majority of the paintings produced during this period when the painter returned to those places of his childhood and early youth which aroused the need to produce 'documents' on them.

This realism, it must be admitted, is no more than episodic. Nor is it a cold and meticulously accurate form of realism, but a realism that is compassionate and moving. It goes without saying that when Chagall speaks of 'documents' he should not be taken too literally. What actually took place during this return was a confrontation with a reality that belonged to former days, a reality from which he had been separated and which had been active in his memory, inspiring intense nostalgia and giving rise to a whole world of strange enchantment. Now all this was there once again, alive, concrete, true and moving. It was above all the people that moved the returning artist: the newspaper vendor, the unforgettable and unchanged old Jews, the beggars with their sacks, the vagabonds, the holy men at prayer, the mumbling, bearded faces, old and lined, and the eternal rabbi with his visage of eternity. The rabbi is caught in the highest degree of perfection in the famous *The Praying Jew – Jew in Black and White* (Ill. *41*), to which the *tallith* – the prayer-shawl with its wide and strict geometry, its stripes, and its brilliant whiteness – confers an impressive and monumental quality. The other ritual objects, even the least of them, also contribute to this plastic effect. Far from distracting and diverting our attention, the *tefillim*, the prayer phylacteries bound to the forehead and the arm by leather straps, are an

42 *Lilies of the Valley*, 1916

43 *Wedding*, 1917. The lovers here are surrounded by the simple, familiar symbols of the angel, the house and the fiddler, while their future child appears in outline on Bella's cheek

integral part of the solemnity of the whole. It is the general effect, and not the details, that captivates us.

The artist was enchanted just as much by nature as by people. It is worth pointing out – and I do not know whether this observation has been made or sufficiently stressed – that the Jewish society into which Chagall was born was a complete one, consisting of both rural and urban elements. Thus he is one of few Jews who could have spoken about 'I and the village', and who could have had tales to tell about it. In his earlier pictures, painted in the cities of Saint Petersburg and Paris, can be seen the power of his memories of Lyozno. He was like a young peasant from the Russian provinces. He would have been familiar with plant life, with cattle and the cattle market, he would have watched unmoved as his grandfather, the butcher, slaughtered the animals – a cruel performance, no doubt, for a tender heart to observe. But his was the heart of a country child, and every country child eats meat and knows that the countryside has its necessary and inescapable laws. We should never overlook this peasant side to Chagall's character, for it accounts for much of the ingenuous and primitive quality of his art, his robustness and his vigour. He is a teller of both fantastic and rustic tales. These two spheres go together; the best story-tellers display a marked connection between them, for both are companions of the animals and the flowers, and are intimate with their profoundest mysteries.

44 *Vitebsk Seen from Mount Zadunov*, 1917. One of a series of pictures of Chagall's native town that must rank among his finest landscapes

45 *The Blue House*, 1917. Another of the Vitebsk landscapes

In Russia Chagall rediscovered nature, and did so with a joy and bliss that was all the more intense since it was linked with the joy of love. He had married Bella on 25th July 1915, and the newly-weds spent their honeymoon at Zaolcha, near Vitebsk, amidst the birches and the pines, beneath a lilac sky. A child, Ida, their cherished Idotchka, was born to them in the spring of 1916 at Saint Petersburg. They had rented a *dacha* in the country and spent the summers of 1916 and 1917 there. In the warmth of this happiness he painted landscapes which may be included among the first documents of his return to Vitebsk and Lyozno, as well as more deliberately composed views of the market, the cemetery and various houses in Vitebsk (*Ill. 45*). And there is his view of Vitebsk from Mount Zadunov (*Ill. 44*), so calm and lovely beneath a vast spread of foliage – 'my sad and joyful town'. This is the town in its very essence, in its tangible and visible reality. All these works express an enchantment with nature which is infectious. Chagall admitted this nature to his soul and his soul loved it. Until that time he had doubtless been unaware to what extent he loved it, and with what kind of innocent and infinite passion. He no longer had to struggle, as he formerly did, to rediscover nostalgic secrets buried in the dreams of his boyhood – his mind, like his body, extended full length in the picture of *The Poet Reclining* (*Ill. 46*), abandoning itself to the joy of those heavenly days at Zaolcha.

46 (*left*) *The Poet Reclining*, 1915. A self-portrait in a rural setting not far from Vitebsk

47 (*above*) *Lovers in Blue*, 1914

48 *Over the Town*, 1917–8. One of the major works produced in Vitebsk during the first winter of the revolution

Chagall's work now expressed the hymn to love in its most radiant form. From the time of their first meeting until their engagement, the figure of Bella had already appeared repeatedly in his canvases, and was always presented in the most graceful and tender form imaginable. Then came the pictures of the kiss, among which there is the *Lovers in Blue* (*Ill. 47*) of 1914, completely bathed in celestial ultramarine; but even more delightful than this, if that were possible, is the series of pictures in which the two profiles are inclined towards each other, no longer in a kiss, but with all the lines complementing each other in a combined movement, an overall proximity that is a symbol of the kiss. In their exquisite melody of line, and their no less exquisite lightness of colouring, these are the purest, the simplest and at the same time the most intense and resounding pictures ever to have issued from the inspiration of love. 'When a man and a woman are together', it is written in the Talmud, 'the Divine Presence dwells amidst them.' In the Zohar, too, it says: 'When desire unites male to female, the universe is blessed, and joy reigns above and below.' Surely this is the union of two beings, occurring at the beginning of all time in the bosom of the One, that we read of in the verse from the *Song of Songs* (II, 6): 'His left hand is under my head, and his right hand embraces me.'

The motif of flight now emerged in full force, justifying the learned interpretations that associate it with love. On a canvas painted in 1914 a bearded beggar is shown flying over snow-covered Vitebsk. But hereafter the sky belongs only to the lovers; it is the scene of their pleasure and jubilation. In *The Birthday* (*Ill. 49*), the

49 *The Birthday*, 1915. The painting depicts Bella bringing flowers for Chagall

50 *Promenade*, 1913

miracle is a domestic one – occurring at the painter's lodgings, in his room, amidst his furniture – and is occasioned by the bunch of flowers brought by his fiancée. Then, after the wedding celebrations, the sky opens up. In *Promenade* (*Ill. 50*) the husband has both feet on the ground, but at arm's length his wife spins around at extra-

51 (*right*) *Double Portrait with Wineglass*, 1917

ordinary heights. In *Over the Town* (*Ill. 48*) he holds her in an embrace and carries her off in a great soaring flight, and everywhere below are the houses of the town like toys. Finally, in the *Double Portrait with Wineglass* (*Ill. 51*) the wife is supporting her husband on her shoulders in a no less extraordinary triumph of love over the laws of gravity and the limits of human strength. The colouring of greens, blues and pinks is fresh and lively and of an infinitely warming tenderness. Gone are the browns and blacks, the livid hues of the early pictures, such as *The Dead Man* and *The Birth* of 1908–10 (*Ills 7, 8*). Yet the pictures of festivals and love which he was now painting are also 'fantastic'. Franz Meyer is right, however, when he says that even these 'fantastic' works are based on the naturalism of the 'documents' and display the same style. The artist's genius was now devoting itself to nature and truth. The motif of flight is an expression of life, and it is in this sense that it may be identified with his need to love, a need which had now been fully and completely satisfied. The dream had become reality.

52 *Street at Night*

CHAPTER FOUR

Russia

Meanwhile events were taking place that constituted another reality. The Russia into which Chagall had re-integrated himself was a Russia at war. Russian soldiers had already featured in the paintings in which he had recorded his memories, but those he painted now were real soldiers that he had actually seen, professional soldiers who went off to war, to fight, to kill and be killed. When they drank, it was not like the traditional tales or songs about soldiers drinking; this was drinking wine in canteens or bivouacs before and after battle. Chagall, like others, was drawn into the vast machine of war and went to work in a military office in Petrograd.

Then came the revolution and Chagall continued to serve Russia. In September 1918 Lunacharsky appointed him Commissar for Art in the government of Vitebsk. He was responsible for the administration of the fine arts in this region, and had to establish academies, schools, studios and museums, to select and appoint teachers, train artists and organize exhibitions. The little Jew hitherto absorbed by dreams limited to his own Jewish community, hitherto confined to a far outpost of a Russia that for him was restricted and bristling with prohibitions, suddenly found himself thrust headlong into a Russia now in the throes of reconstruction and consequently offering boundless opportunities. Vitebsk was both his Jewish and his Russian home town. Vitebsk represented his childhood in the ghetto and at the same time represented the whole of his vast, unfamiliar, adored, terrifying though longed-for Russia. This Vitebsk was granted and entrusted to him by the revolution. Suddenly he found himself promoted to the role of one of its most eminent personalities and in his own sphere, that of the artist, he was to assume control and

53 *Wounded Soldier*, 1914

54 *Young Soldiers*, 1914

55 *Wounded Soldier*, 1914

responsibility for it. For the activities of the artist may consist not merely in engaging his own creative faculties and solving his own aesthetic problems, in evolving his art and producing his *œuvre*, it may also extend to enterprises in which art becomes a social affair, a thing to be taught, to be encouraged, broadcast, exhibited, to be communicated and applied, a thing in which to interest the people and to grace public occasions.

Here Chagall had come to the climax of his adventure. He had returned to his native land in search of his memories, and from being just a part of his memories embodied in a few poetic images this homeland of his now grew to assume the proportions of a whole new, dynamic life, a life suddenly permitting him to pursue his work in all directions and on every level. He had been moved at the idea of seeing Russia again, and now here she was in the midst of activity, engaged in making history, in a state of upheaval that had its repercussions throughout the world. And now he had been drawn into this upheaval and called upon to participate in it. Was there any limit to the opportunities life held, was there any limit to his own potentialities? And he was involved in private action as well as collective action, for he had found the most decisive moment of his destiny as a man, the happiness of love. Moreover, at this time his importance as an artist was recognized in Russia. From that time on Chagall was at one with himself and with the world.

At one with himself, for it seemed as if all his inner conflicts had really been resolved. All the subjects and faces that had been a part of his life, and were so fascinating to the outsider, now simply became the plastic elements in his great work.

At one with the world, for now he was part of the world and of society. Love had given him the key to happiness. Love had convinced him that it was good to be part of society. All the peculiarities of his social condition had been eliminated. The return to his homeland, to the land of his childhood and his childhood dreams, had coincided with such extraordinary circumstances that all difficulties had vanished, including the difficulty of knowing himself to be a

56 *The Traveller*, 1917

Jew and thus not being able to regard himself as Russian. Also, without previously having denied his origins, he now entered into a
different realm of existence, that of freedom.

All this emphasizes the fact that there is one word – liberty –
which provides the key to the mystery of his youthful painting. All
these fantasies of space and flight, these soarings and wanderings and
extravagances, all these metamorphoses of dreams and desires, all
these metaphors in a new and singular plastic language express
liberty. Henceforth man is master in the choice of his abode, in
establishing himself wherever he chooses in the world, just as the
painter is master of his vocabulary, his symbols and his art.

57 *The Acrobat*, 1914

One immediate result of this liberty is the sudden change in the scope and output of Chagall's activity during the Russian Revolution now that the latter had accepted him, invested him with great authority and called upon him to participate in history. He had to shake off his previous social condition and expand, which is the first step towards feeling free and making oneself ready for everything that the world may expect. A free man is one who is a part of the common, general condition – for him it is not so much a matter of what he does, but of facing up to reality.

The realities which faced Chagall the painter were most exciting, difficult and fraught with disappointments. The problems of administering artistic affairs is the most arduous task imaginable, particularly when tackled in the course of a proletarian revolution and violent upheavals destined to lead to the establishment of a socialist régime. Yet the initial excitement must have persisted and even predominated for a long while. Enthusiasm for the revolution had come to a head at a time when a revolutionary fire was also spreading throughout poetry and art. There were young poets and artists of genius, pioneers, new schools, controversies, manifestos, a whole surge of new artistic theories corresponding to those arising in Germany, Italy and Paris. The revolution could not but favour these movements, and invited the artists active in them to form organizations and committees along the lines of those being set up to cover all sections of labour. It encouraged mass demonstrations and celebrations, commissioned the decoration of its halls and monuments, and finally promoted the creation of a style that was to be the art of the emerging society, calling for the kind of work that the people could recognize as its own art. Art in the streets! – this was the order of the day, and it did not seem impossible at the time. On the contrary, it was felt that a social revolution must inevitably be accompanied by a revolution in art. The same underlying principle was common to both: rejection of the past coupled with advance into the future.

All the spontaneous and generous emotions of the artist's soul must have readily responded to the great revolution, liberating man

58 *Man Carrying Street*

from enslavement and injustice, and above all liberating him from the acceptance of enslavement and injustice, consequently restoring his self-respect and enabling him to attain a supreme condition of fulfilment and harmony. Amidst such prodigious changes there was no doubt whatever that art and artists had their role to play. Everything was in the process of adjustment to new principles, to a new régime, a new spirit, new ends. Everything was being re-organized, including artistic life. Chagall, as Commissar for Art, had much to do and was constantly rushing to Moscow to present his grievances and requests to the higher authorities. He also had his difficulties with other artists, their dogmas, theories and sects.

Yet at the opening of the Vitebsk Academy a poet recited an ode to Chagall. Chagall was famous and admired. But no sooner had he turned his back to go off on one of those expeditions to Moscow, in order to extract a few additional roubles for his Academy, than the Suprematists stepped in and took his place. On his return he found them established in his Academy. But the more turbulent factions of the *avant-garde* were not all he had to contend with, for as was only to be expected there were also the dull-witted representatives of the revolution itself. All régimes have their bigots and they never fail to make their presence felt. Nor is this purely a matter of *bourgeois* or *non-bourgeois*, Marxist or non-Marxist, it is the same ignorance the world over. Never-ending questions rang in Chagall's ears, bringing him to the point of exhaustion, exasperation and disgust, yet he could not ignore them for they came from his colleagues as well as from one-time firemen in the old régime: 'Why is the cow green? And why does the horse fly in the sky?'

After this experiment in Vitebsk Chagall submitted to another experiment, this time in Moscow, at the heart of the revolution, the heart of eternal Russia. It, too, was an experiment aimed at integrating art with collective life; but it was less critical and contradictory, and this time it took place not under the extreme and exceptional conditions of the revolution, but within a traditional framework, the theatre. For in every age and among all peoples and all régimes the theatre has always been the art of collective expression, the art of the people. Since art was now exclusively of the people, it was only natural that Chagall should turn to the theatre, the art of the people *par excellence*.

At the time of his first stay in Saint Petersburg, and again while he was commissar in Vitebsk, he had sketched designs for stage sets and costumes. But he was able to begin designing in earnest when he came into contact with the Kamerny State Jewish Theatre from Petrograd which had settled in Moscow in 1920 with Alexis Granowsky as its manager.

The Russians have always had a passion for the theatre. The Russian genius naturally inclines towards comedy and spectacle, and has an instinctive feeling for dramatic action, argument, invective, gestures, dance and rhythm, combined with decorative beauty. And on the level of histrionic expression the Jewish genius is very much

59 Costume design for *The Miniatures* by Sholem Aleichem

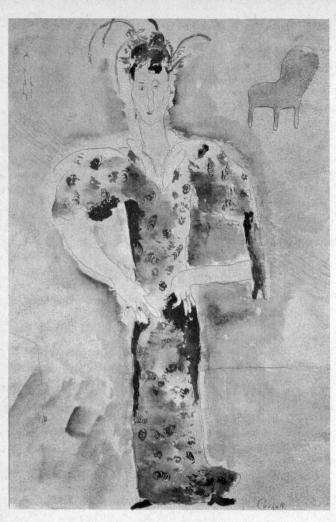

60 One of Chagall's
illustrations for Gogol's
Dead Souls

akin to it. Russia has long been fertile soil for great men of the
theatre. At this time Tairoff, Stanislavsky and Meyerhold had already
made their names. The latter two were pursuing directly opposed
objectives, one advocating a true-to-life naturalism and the other a
stylized form of theatre; Chagall could not help championing the
second cause. It is not surprising that his designs for Synge's *Playboy
of the Western World* were rejected by one of the directors of Stanislavsky's theatre on the grounds of being anti-naturalist. On the
other hand, Alexis Granowsky complained about the naturalism of

his style. However, once he had entrusted Chagall with the first presentation – some 'miniatures' by Shalom Aleichem (*Ill. 59*) – he realized that it was essential to give the artist free reign. By contrast, when Wachtangoff, director of the Habimah, the other Jewish theatre, asked him to help to stage the *Dybbuk*, a hopeless conflict ensued. Wachtangoff was a pupil of Stanislavsky and intended to stay faithful to his master.

Whether they were used or not, Chagall's designs for sets and costumes must be regarded as an important landmark in the history of stage design, leading towards emancipation from strict realism, towards a fresh and constantly revised concept of space. Here Chagall was in his element; his plastic conception of space could be put to practical purpose. His characteristic method of using space was to

61 Scene design for Gogol's *The Inspector General*

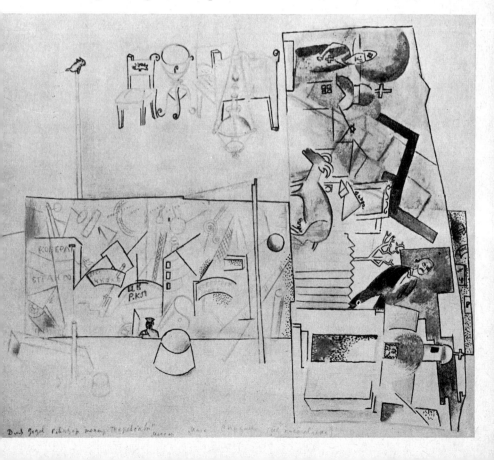

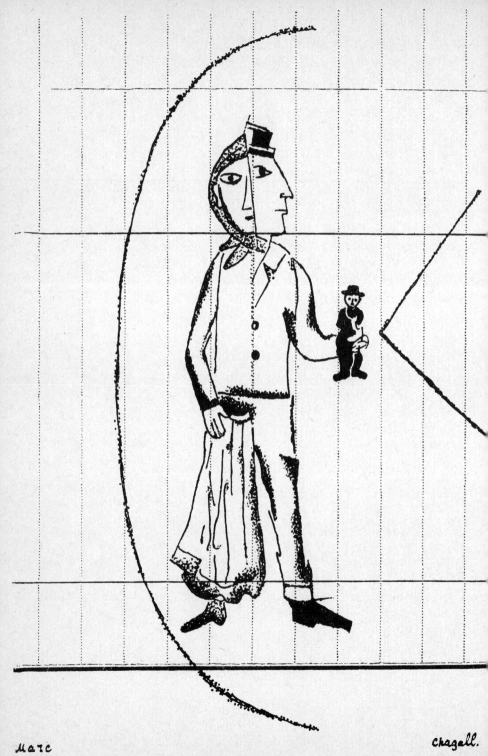

Chagall.

build it up in all its dimensions, providing a structure for living characters and all kinds of concrete objects to catch hold of, to hang from, to climb about on. Moreover, this use of space could divide up the stage and make it appear smaller or higher than it actually was. There is a gaiety and playful vitality about all these creations, and the artist was able to enjoy the additional pleasure of sharing it with a crowd of spectators, the audience assembled for the great dramatic communion. Crazy geometry, aggressive costumes and colours – all the means he employed transcend the art of the painter and go beyond pure design. They constitute the true art of stage design and production, enabling the art of the actor and the author to be realized. Chagall identified himself with each separate performance: he not only provided the framework, but with all the expansive energy of his genius he enacted and consummated the spectacle.

Chagall's activity was not confined to the stage itself, it reached into the auditorium and the foyer. *Love on the Stage*, the four great *Murals* and the *Introduction to the Jewish Theatre* are essentially theatrical in spirit, heightening the effect on the spectators produced by the illusion and marvels of the performance. Chagall expended the greatest verve and energy on these works. The absolute freedom of expression which the theatre provided brings us to another of the major features of Chagall's character – his humour. His *joie de vivre*, the delight at being in all points of space at one and the same time, at making space one's own is no intellectual pleasure, but a physical, organic pleasure that possesses the whole being, and must therefore end in the physical, organic phenomenon that possesses the entire being: laughter. We may consider it as a spiritual phenomenon, both physical and metaphysical, which was how Baudelaire saw it.

Chagall is a profoundly comic buffoon of a genius. We have already touched upon the comic element in the most complex and poetic of his works, those in which memories of his earliest days appear in such strange forms. These are forms which produce laughter in the theatre – and in the circus too, another of Chagall's favourite subjects, where everything is turned upside-down. Things or people upside-down are a great source of laughter. Indeed the plays staged by Chagall were mostly comedies, and if some of them had their tragic side it was a whimsical kind of tragedy that borders on the burlesque. Among the authors of these plays Gogol can perhaps best illustrate this ambiguity. In the spring of 1919 Chagall had been approached by a small experimental theatre in Petrograd to design the sets for two works by Gogol. A few months later a Moscow theatre known as the Theatre of Revolutionary Satire (*Terevsat*), whose director was Razume, asked Chagall to design the sets and costumes for *The Inspector General* (*Ill. 61*). These were Chagall's first encounters with Gogol. Others followed, and one of these is of major importance in Chagall's work, namely the illustration of *Dead Souls*. Gogol and Chagall are undeniably kindred spirits. The resemblances are marked between Chagall's *vis comica* and Gogol's, which is typically Russian – capricious, extremist, loaded with pathos, a lyrical form of caricature that brought things into relief. And in presentation it was essentially theatrical. But Gogol's concept of humour could equally well have been Chagall's. This Russian buffoonery linked the two men, and it was by way of Gogol that Chagall returned to the very heart of Russia, showing how fundamentally Russian he was.

After Chagall's return to his own country we see him at his most characteristic. I have tried to avoid describing these characteristic features *a priori* in abstract terms. An artist's work, like his personality, develops as the circumstances and experiences of his early life become assimilated into material that can be drawn upon. We must therefore re-consider this experience in order to discover in it the essential factor that biographers never attempt to reveal: vocation.

CHAPTER FIVE

Vocation

Chagall is a painter, and nothing that relates to his inner life and outward life would be of the slightest interest if these two lives had not been translated into paintings. We have described the adventure, the marvellous odyssey of his childhood impressions; this exists only in his pictures and is valid only because of them. 'In short, this is painting', he declares in *My Life*, in the passage where he describes his half-dozen uncles, how some looked like this, others like that, some had black beards, others had brown beards. And thereupon, he says quite abruptly, 'In short, this is painting.' It is painting, nothing but painting, and everything always leads back to painting. He has repeated time and again that he has no interest in anything else. So let us turn to this.

Of all the events in Chagall's childhood the most significant was his decision to become a painter. We have already told how the child's first declarations were received, and how things did not go his way to begin with. But finally he won the day, and became a painter. But what kind of painter? At the very beginning he produced exercises in a dull and heavy, well-meaning naturalism, and we still have a few examples of this work. Even so, in these earliest beginnings the vocation to paint very soon became the vocation to paint in a particular way. The young boy could not have wanted to paint without wanting to produce his own kind of painting. Chagall has repeatedly maintained that he wished to paint in a manner that was not realist. He assures us that, right from the start, he abhorred realism. This illustrates the most profound, stubborn and capricious side of his nature, rebelling against the laws of permanence governing things and refusing to accept their sovereignty even to the point of contradiction. The first thing he does is to reverse these laws, to push them aside and send them toppling down.

It is not long before this provocative spirit of protest makes itself felt. In 1911, for example, he confronts us with the *Yellow Room* (*Ill. 63*) and the picture curiously entitled *The Drunkard* (*Ill. 64*). In both of these canvases we see a table. Now a table is the very model of stability, but there is a dizzy lack of balance about these tables. The bottles and other objects on them appear to have been overcome by seasickness. But even in the earliest years, during 1908 and 1909, there is a manifest desire to contradict reality. Desire is perhaps the wrong word, for the artist works by instinct, and the passionate independence of his work is an aspect of his passionate nature. This passion is pure artlessness and the means employed is artless-

63 *The Yellow Room*, 1911. In this painting, for the first time, the dominant colour is a basic element in the work

64 *The Drunkard*, 1911–2. Even at this early stage in Chagall's career he was trying to emphasize the spontaneous inspiration

ness; his painting is naïve. Generally speaking, painters of whom this term is used submit to things. Chagall's naïvety, on the other hand, consists in opposing things – that is its purpose. Thus, in the years 1908 and 1909, without any deliberate or calculated intention, but simply because it was the way that was natural to him, the trees in the lanes and the chairs in the parlours were painted crooked and at crazy angles, executed in uncertain strokes. And in this way his works quite suddenly acquired a highly personal, unmistakable quality without parallel. They are inescapably 'naïve' as well as thoroughly unusual, as in *The Dead Man* (*Ill. 7*), whose content and setting I have discussed at length.

This originality in his work was the outcome of an entire mental process that has already been analysed. I should add that this process was accomplished by a painter who was amazingly precocious. Already in full possession of his faculties as a painter, he knew what kind of a painter he was and what kind of paintings he was going to produce: paintings that were in no way realistic, but which were the product of his own personal fantasies, inner impulses and all that occurs in the depths of the heart. That these occurrences are likely to be most strange and mysterious is proven by *The Dead Man*. Yet these mysteries are, like everything else, translated with the same innocent and clumsy simplicity. And it is from this clumsiness and innocence that he derives his confidence when he speaks of his painting and its aims, and the particular direction he intends to follow.

The language he uses, too, is highly individual. Chagall differs from other painters in the things he speaks of; he uses the terms of the common language they speak in a different sense. When they speak of dimension, he speaks of 'psychic dimension'; when they speak of 'means', he speaks of 'illogical' or, again, of 'psychic means'. Naturally, they also speak of space, the great hobby horse of all painters. Here again his meaning and intention are quite unique. We have seen that, with all the force of his child-like imagination, he strives after a very different kind of space in which to place his forms, objects and characters. 'How', he asked himself while he was composing *The Dead Man*, 'could I paint a street with psychic forms but without literature?' This was an assertion of his distrust of literature. A literary painter is not afraid to portray his subject by means of a 'psychic form' as a way of representing it on the psychic level, that is by means of a symbol or an allegory, and he sets about this task in a deliberate fashion. But this is not Chagall's purpose; he is not a literary painter. His forms may be 'psychic' forms, but they are still essentially forms, and as such integrate quite naturally into a plastic creation.

This resolutely anti-realist intention, though never evident except in his painting, predetermined the unique course his future work was to take, singling him out for an inflexible destiny and assuring him an unwavering originality. This anti-realism is in itself a simple enough idea. In the mind of Chagall it takes on an extraordinary vigour and makes the paradoxical demand that a psychic reality be presented through painting. This plastic representation would be not only a transposition of psychic reality, but also a psychic representation, thanks to some unknown form of identification or transubstantiation.

Where the goals are difficult of attainment, the work that issues from such ambition must bear the stamp of separateness and necessarily occupy an isolated position. It does not bear classification. Yet despite its isolation it will become the choice of the greatest number. Born of a spiritual exercise on a spiritual level, it will attract the spiritual mind. The ambition which has produced this art, the art of Chagall, which by its content and its means is a spiritual, magical art, *ars magna*, can be considered, appreciated and admired only in a manner particular to itself, one which involves a great deal of love.

Dominated by his vocation, entirely aware of the singularity of the existence to which it destined him and which might well remain unfulfilled – although it did in fact lead to astonishing fulfilment – the young Chagall was impatient to go further afield. The impatience he felt, together with what amounted to a spiritual compulsion, was occasioned by his need to paint. He had to paint. Everything came down to this one necessity. But how could it be satisfied in such limited places as Vitebsk or even Saint Petersburg? One suffocated and languished there, with nothing and no one to inspire one to paint. Inevitably, the young Chagall was caught up in the great whirlwind that has swept so many others with compelling vocations towards Paris. For there one can paint, and one does paint.

At this point I cannot help feeling justified in my initial cavalier dismissal of the details concerning Chagall's origins, his family, his milieu, etc., and in having selected only what could have been absorbed into his work, in having picked out not those details that could have affected his work, but the ones that took effect within it, that made it breathe and brought it to life. Obviously one must take into account the painter's attachment to the places, things and people of his home environment, as well as the emotions experienced at the time of his return to Russia and throughout all the circumstances attendant upon this return. But is it not striking to see how readily this bond slackened and at what point it occurred? However intense these human ties may have been, they were of little significance for the painter's real existence. In fact it was no great hardship for him to uproot himself, for his vocation as a painter was the arbiter of his destiny. Thus he was being his true self when he impatiently rejected all the picturesque features of his origins, the very elements which have been claimed as the clue to his work but which merely cloud the issue. Above all else, it was his painting that mattered.

What he had left behind lived on in his mind and became the source of intense emotions – emotions that were felt in his heart but, more important, were absorbed by the genius of a creative artist. They inspired his great hymn to humanity. This hymn embodies his vocation, and it is this vocation towards which the whole of Chagall the man is orientated. Once we have realized this, it becomes evident that the dominant part of Chagall the man is Chagall the painter.

The history of the painter and his vocation form a continuous accompaniment to the progress of his career which has so far been described; the history of the painter is sustained by the history of the man. Man's life, his career and his progress are all parts of a well-defined cradle, the source to which they return after various stages on the journey before setting out afresh. These stages are all a part of vocation, each contributing to its fulfilment. For vocation is the main thing. This explains how, despite his human involvement, the poet has the faculty of detachment, the ability to project himself into space like the people in his paintings. Here are his own words:

> Mine alone is the land
> that exists in my soul.
> I enter it without a passport
> like I do my own home.

65 *Little Parlour*, 1908, an early instance of Chagall's striking use of colour

All other lands have frontiers and formalities to be observed. But the land where he feels most at home is his own inner land, the mysterious place in which his irrepressible vocation takes shape. Further on in the poem, his only authentic declaration of allegiance, he continues:

> *Gardens blossom within me.*
> *My flowers are invented.*
> *The streets are mine,*
> *but there are no houses.*
> *They have been gone since childhood,*
> *their inhabitants wander through the air*
> *in search of a home.*
> *They live in my soul...*

99

So here he was in Paris. The important thing now is to show how Chagall's art – with its purpose, its specific problems, its secret mechanisms and its unshakable naïvety – was able to resist the intermingling of talents in the great melting-pot of Paris. This was the home of painting, which at that time was at its zenith. These talents were being deployed in diverse and adventurous directions by young artists, some of whom came from far afield, while others were native to France. Together they made up one of the most brilliant generations ever to have emerged. Chagall found himself immediately accepted by this struggling world that lived its Bohemian life on the fringe of society, confident in its own boldness and justified by its impending success and glory. These painters were producing many different kinds of work, but out of this variety two principal movements emerged: Fauvism and, hard upon its heels, Cubism. Chagall, although he was accepted as part of this magnificent array of talent, managed to keep his individuality so that his contribution continued to be unique.

Many of his works from this first Parisian period reflect the revolutionary plastic technique that was causing such a sensation at the time. Right from the start Chagall had shown himself to be a dazzling colourist – brilliant, vigorous, arbitrary, eternally unpredictable, and delightful even in the harshness and crudity of his colours – so that it is often tempting to include him among the Fauvists. Even before he came to Paris he could have been described as a Fauvist for such paintings as his *Little Parlour* (*Ill. 65*) of 1908. The yellow sheet of sky in the *Dead Man* (*Ill. 7*) might also be regarded as a Fauvist flash of humour. He arrived in Paris just as the dazzling flame of Fauvism was burning itself out, and yet he could not help giving himself up whole-heartedly to his Fauvist inclinations. Among his discoveries in Paris was the work of Van Gogh, who may have been known in Russia but it was in Paris that his ideas were being put into practice in all their blazing radiance. Here there were not only provocative paintings to be seen, but in the very air he breathed, the air that bathed all things in its light, there was for him an indescribable brilliance, warmth, electricity, potential energy and pleasure – a light that dazzled the young painter and which he described as '*lumière liberté*'.

This light opened his eyes. He has often recalled how sad and mournful the light had always seemed to him in Russia. The light of Paris, the 'light of freedom', illuminates those paintings produced in 1910 during that first year of what has been generally acknowledged as Chagall's so-called Fauvist period: *The Harvest* (*Ill. 66*), with its riot of blue foliage and its deliberate emphasis on yellow and vermilion; *The Studio* (*Ill. 67*), which, with what seems like impetuous clumsiness, is in even greater contrast to the *Little Parlour* of his Russian years; *The Model* (1910), with its brilliant contrasts of darkness and light; and *The Wedding* (1910), with its joyful medley of colours.

However, we must beware of over-estimating the Fauvist influence in these paintings, nor can we regard their creator as won over to Fauvism. The truth is that Chagall has always been and always will be a Fauvist, and the effect of Fauvism, as a Parisian movement that happened to be current at that time, was essentially to activate and heighten Chagall's own intrinsic tendencies as a colourist. The revolution of Fauvism corresponded to Chagall's highly personal preference for colour applied in an autonomous way. Moreover Fauvism was not the only contemporary movement with which Chagall found himself in natural harmony; the same applied to expressionism. Indeed, one often refers to Chagall's expressionism. But it never occurred to Chagall to declare that he supported any of these theories. If he did, it was not for any intellectual motive, but instinctively with his whole being. This is inevitable with every kind of painting that, instead of being based upon a system, consists of powerful demonstrations of our sensory motor system, of organic impulses carried to the limits of our powers of expression and imagination.

Chagall's relationship to Cubism is quite a different matter. Chagall encountered Cubism when he arrived in Paris. He could not

66 *The Harvest*, 1910. An excellent example of Chagall's Fauvist phase in Paris

remain indifferent to it, and was to some extent influenced by it. Here one is justified in speaking of influence, or at least of some degree of assimilation. Yet this geometric and rational revolution was completely foreign to Chagall's temperament. This explains the self-conscious element in the paintings that incline towards Cubism, as for example in the *Still Life* (*Ill. 29*) in the Erick Estorick collection in London, or the *Poet*, also known as *Half-Past Three* (*Ill. 72*), and the *Adam and Eve* (1912, *Ill. 73*) in the St Louis Museum, which gives a disagreeably affected impression. The Cubist reticulation in both the *Seated Nude*, a gouache, and in *The Soldier Drinks* (*Ill. 71*), both painted in 1911, is stiff and rather forced. The same technique is used in *Self-portrait with Seven Fingers* (*Ill. 68*), but here it combines happily with the charms of the poetic imagination, the

wit and the colouring of Chagall at his best. The supreme example
of Chagall's Cubist work is his *Homage to Apollinaire* (*Ill. 70*), in
which he wished to pay tribute to the poet who had appointed himself as the interpreter and champion of Cubism. The composition of
this picture is in fact geometric, consisting of a circle divided up by
radii. The circle is broken in places, and encloses other circles or
segments of concentric circles. Against this background stands the
couple, Adam and Eve, issuing from one and the same pair of legs,
their trunks separating at the very centre of the circular composition.
Such a work can hardly be called Cubist, since it is not a homoge-
neous composition in the way that the *Adam and Eve* of 1912 is.

67 *Studio*, 1910. This work, depicting Chagall's room in the Impasse du Maine,
is one of the major works of his first Paris period

68 *Self-portrait with Seven Fingers*, 1912. The first of the series of portraits from the Paris period

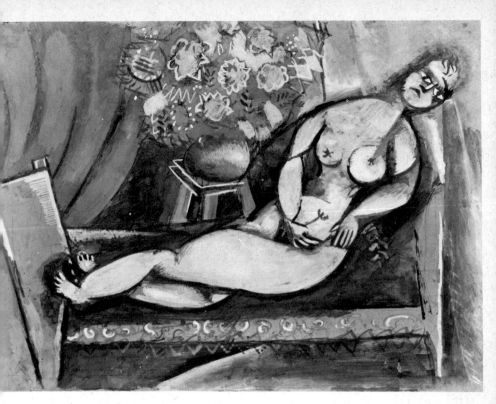

69 *Reclining Nude*, 1911

Geometry is here employed solely to compose a background, and is thus purely decorative. It would be more appropriate to place this work alongside that of Delaunay, who was to produce his *Discs* and *Circular Forms* in the following year. On closer inspection, the circular background of *Homage to Apollinaire*, with the red segment on the left and the grey or dark tones in the segments on the right, seems to be not so much an expression of the constructional and rational problems of Cubism as a foreshadowing of the work of Delaunay in which a cosmic feeling reigns supreme. Chagall is clearly using a geometric scheme here, and certainly he does so with great facility (we know that as a child he was very good at geometry at school), but it is quite different from that of orthodox Cubism in the way it approaches the cosmic lyricism of his friend Delaunay. The circular nucleus of his *Homage to Apollinaire* is the sun, our source of light, dispensing the colours of the prism and ordaining the rhythm of our existence and the alternation between day and night. Indeed, one might suggest that this tribute to Apollinaire was not addressed to him as the interpreter of Cubism, but rather as the father of Orphism, which he subsequently became. In the following year, 1912, Apollinaire together with Delaunay used this name to grace the heresy which exalted light, colour and natural forces above all objective reality.

Chagall was familiar with these natural forces and cultivated them. They responded to his sensuality, to his vitality, to his genius and to this praise of the human couple and of love which he knew from his religious tradition. In short this picture – a picture of singular majesty and deservedly famous – must be recognized as an example of the symbolism peculiar to Chagall, which derives consciously or unconsciously from the cosmology and fundamental sexualism of the Zohar. Scholars tell us that already in the *Eyn-Sof*, the 'Without End' – an insoluble paradox in itself – there is the distinction of the male being springing up from the right-hand side and the female from the left. But on these points, and on others related to this symbolism, I cannot do better than to refer the reader to an excellent section in Franz Meyer's exhaustive work, *Marc Chagall*, Thames and Hudson, London 1964.

Chagall lived and worked among these theories that were springing up in the Paris of this privileged era. Some of them appealed to him and seemed to coincide with what he was trying to do; others contradicted his own efforts but still intrigued and tempted him and he would have liked to make use of them. However, as might be expected, this led to results that were unsatisfactory and superficial. When, as we see in his *Homage to Apollinaire*, he uses geometric forms, they have nothing to do with Cubist geometric forms, but

70 *Homage to Apollinaire*, 1911–2. Also a homage to Canudo, Cendrars and Walden, whose names appear with Apollinaire's round the heart, this is Chagall's most important painting up to this date. Both in its deployment of geometrical forms and its biblical symbolism of Adam and Eve with the apple, it is a milestone in the painter's development. (Note that the numbers on the left of the outer circle correspond to the numbers 9, 10 and 11 on a clock face.)

respond to inner demands of a quite different order. The fragmentation of *I and the Village* (*Ill. 12*), that work fundamental to the universe of Chagall, might appear analogous to the reticulation of some of the masters of Cubism. In reality this merely provides a means of distributing the various figures of Chagall's imaginary world by means of an ideal and fantastic use of space. Henceforth it is no longer a Cubist process, methodically applied; it is a poetic and specifically 'Chagallian' process. The large triangle on the left with its point at the centre is no longer an element in the construction, it is the profile of a cow; the other triangle merely serves to outline a tree laden with round fruit. The section that stands out at the top on the right is no longer part of the construction, but a piece of Chagall's poetic world, with a *moujik* walking, a scythe over his shoulder, and next to him a woman upside-down. Thus, although the painting is geometric, it is not a geometric reticulation of reality in the Cubist sense, but a convenient, amusing and comic arrangement of unreality, of that dream-like, remembered, transfigured, poetic and – as he called it – *psychic* universe that is Chagall's.

Thus, in some of the works produced during this Parisian period, while the artist's creative spirit was receiving many and varied stimuli, we may detect instances of assimilation that are intuitive and not explicitly formulated and yet which remain in keeping with the intimate and inalienable nature of the artist. On the other hand, we find artificial and self-conscious borrowings that go contrary to this same nature. In order to study these borrowings one could examine certain of Chagall's works, especially those produced between 1911 and 1912, and discover in them a number of features that are analogous to the works of Delaunay, and of Gleizes or Metzinger, or even to Léger's *The Wedding*. One might also refer to certain Futurist works although Chagall has clearly stated his own antipathy towards the Futurists. But, whether deliberate and plainly stated or implicit and confined to attempts at assimilation, these divergences merged into the general enthusiasm and effervescence of the period – every-

71 *The Soldier Drinks*, 1912. Here the individual forms are more angular, with sharper edges, than in Chagall's previous Cubist paintings

thing, no matter what it was, seemed new, and everything contributed to the great riot of innovation.

We must also remember that this first Parisian period of Chagall's did not solely reflect reactions to the innovations of the moment and his more or less felicitous attempts to adapt himself to various kinds of work. The year 1911 was also the time of the cycle of fantastic poems in which, as we have seen, the secret forces of Chagall's genius were most surprisingly expressed. There were also other works which were possibly less fundamental but no less surprising. All this was doubtless of little significance in relation to the doctrines that were being evolved and the discussions that were dominating the artistic scene. Critics and colleagues alike were struck mainly by the child-like and primitive aspects of Chagall's work. This, too, elicited recognition and praise, and joined the swelling chorus that was transforming the sensibilities of the century.

Guillaume Apollinaire, the poet and prophet of this century, was also guided more by intuition than by theories. He was a man born to seize in his hands elemental forces and, like a magician, to control them and extract the maximum from them. Clearly he was a genius who was capable of reason. He was searching for order and longing to invent, of all things, a form of classicism. But a large part of his genius and his mission – and who can say that it was not the most vital part? – was his lyricism which drew close to Chagall's domain of isolation and innocence.

There have been many descriptions of Apollinaire's visit to Chagall's studio, of how the poet was stupefied and speechless, and then overcome by a fit of uncontrollable hilarity, finally uttering the word 'Supernatural'! An oracular and illuminating utterance which ensured instant communication between the poet and the painter. In one word the poet had seized upon what was absolutely essential to the painter, which the latter had himself always been searching for and had wanted to express if only he had known how. This was what Chagall had meant when, in his own limited and headstrong

72 (*right*) *The Poet*, 1911. Developed from earlier portrait studies of the poet Mazin, the figure in this work has been given a rotated head like that of the woman in *The Yellow Room* (*Ill.* 63)

way, he had said that he loathed realism. He saw this enslavement to reality not only in the avowed realists such as Courbet, but even among the Cubists, who were none the less arousing his curiosity. From the poet there had come a description of the painter that was utterly appropriate, the very word to describe him, the *shem* to be stamped on his forehead. And for his part, in pronouncing this word the poet had described himself, too, and revealed himself to himself. For the power of the word used in such circumstances extends not only to the person to whom it is applied, but also to the person who pronounces it. In applying the epithet *supernatural* to the paintings of Chagall, Apollinaire also applied it to himself and to his poems.

This brings me back to an earlier point, that Apollinaire was more than a highly perceptive and lucid critic, aesthete and philosopher who understood the art of his time and its daring better than anyone (especially those bold enterprises in which the speculative spirit was uppermost and which he himself had dubbed 'scientific Cubism'). Even in the most intelligent and intellectual aspects of the art of his time, Apollinaire perceived a lyricism, a feeling, an impetus, some kind of organic, vital desire for risk, for extravagance, for braving the limits. This was the mood that enlivened the period as a whole, and in particular those other trends represented by less intellectual and systematic figures, who were, however, truly lyrical, intuitive, imaginative, and who none the less aspired to the supernatural.

All of Apollinaire's poetry – in other words, the most fundamental part of him – followed this direction. In one of his last poems, *Collines*, one of those in which the prophetic spirit is strongest, he said:

> *I have finally broken away*
> *from all things natural.*

This was the aim of his quest and his journey. And it is the aim itself that interests us, not its object. This does not imply the least belief in transcendence, but simply reflects a feeling of indifference and disrespect for reality, a feeling of rebellion against it, a longing to break

73 (*right*) *Adam and Eve*, 1912

its laws, a passionate desire to restore to the world of reality its sa-vour, its secret, its inspiration, its being, to revive the significance which would otherwise have perished in the endeavour to remain within the appointed order. Thus this new universe which the imag-ination sought was to be an eloquent, melodious, expressive universe. And so as he stood in front of the painter's works, Guillaume Apol-linaire was profoundly moved. It was a moment when two geniuses were in perfect harmony. On the following day the poet sent the painter his poem *Rotsoge*, improvised on the back of a Chez Baty menu, which was to appear in the issue of the *Soirées de Paris* on 15th April 1914, and subsequently in the *Sturm* magazine's issue of 14th May, as the introduction to an exhibition held the following month. And it was taken up once again in his own *Calligrammes* under the title, 'Through Europe':

> But your hair is the trolley
> that runs through Europe
> clad in little multi-coloured fires.

Poets, like painters, handle colours and images, and can thus establish a mutual understanding concerning unexpected and new ways of seeing things. Poets like Canudo, Salmon and Max Jacob were all friends of Chagall, and above all there was that other great poet, who came possibly even closer to the painter than did Apollinaire, Blaise Cendrars. These men contributed to the lyricism of the period before the war one of the most powerful, original, exciting and im-passioned examples of lyricism ever to have arisen in France in the whole course of her intellectual history. In both its plastic and its verbal forms this lyricism appears fragmentary and discontinuous; its impact is achieved by successive shocks in sound and colour, each of them violent and intense and completely unexpected, and totally unrelated to anything else. And since they do not follow any logical sequence, space is not relevant to them.

To lyricism of this kind space can only be an element, an element in which to immerse itself. Space is limitless – like time, it is 'a river without banks'. This makes space alluring, and the departure attractive. Departure is enough to fill the consciousness with infinite joy. No thought of aim or direction is involved. Departure alone, an impetus and an irresistible urge towards exuberance and expansion. Speed also has its part in this, but not along any road or towards any goal. Consequently it is not so much speed as a violent intensification of rhythms, frenetic rhythms that are forever being cut short and dispersed. No doubt there are things to be seen along these interrupted journeys, things one can never stop to examine or grasp, whose presence is registered like a flash, like the wind on one's cheek. So in a series of consecutive, incoherent, flash-like images the whole planet passes by in all its variegation, with all its possibilities of change and progress. Today makes way for tomorrow, while the past merges indistinctly with the present. Chagall's past did not bear fruit until it was turned into memories, until he had moved on to another place. Everything and everyone is displaced and rootless, fleeting and autonomous. Apollinaire gathered together his scattered roots in the affirmation that he was a French poet and a French soldier (which he proved by giving France his cosmopolitan blood). It should be remembered, however, that the beauty of this poet's verse owes some of its lustre to his gipsy wanderings in the forests of the Ardennes. Cendrars, too, escaped from the confinement of his native Switzerland and chose a life of travel through two continents, singing its praises in his writings, without the refinements and the preciousness of Apollinaire, and in certain material examples similar to the collages of his Cubist friends. And he entered into the hurly-burly of the world with his whole being:

Tell me, Blaise, are we far from Montmartre?

One is always far from Montmartre, far from everywhere. When the traveller does return home to old Montmartre in old Paris, he meets other travellers there – a microcosm containing all the chance arrivals and the strange wanderers of the whole wide world, a breeding ground for every kind of eccentricity.

This lyricism of the wanderer, issuing from a knowledge of the world and acting as its mirror – a *speculum mundi*, in which images merge and follow each other, a magic, cinematographic mirror – is a gay, revelling, swaggering, vital lyricism, truly in step with the world. Yet it is also melancholic, for knowledge breeds melancholy – Dürer was one of many to have discovered this. One cannot miss the melancholy in this lyricism, a profound melancholy, the sadness of accumulated riches, the sadness induced by a surfeit of memories and aspirations and by the excess baggage accumulated through life. It is sadness at the many treasures furtively acquired, carelessly squandered, dispersed and lost, the sadness that comes from insecurity and perpetual farewells, the sadness at the impermanence of all things, and the knowledge that everything involves change and being uprooted from one's surroundings.

This two-fold lyricism, in its cosmic enthusiasm and sad reveries, its prophetic hopes and gloomy presentiments, is the lyricism of youth on the threshold of the apocalypse known to us as the twentieth century.

This then is Chagall's lyricism and the essence of his painting. Because his painting is lyrical he found himself in close accord with the poets of pre-1914 Paris and with the poetry of the time, and with all that could stir the heart and kindle the imagination. This also explains why, apart from a few minor exceptions, he remained unaffected by the theoretical innovations in the painting of the time. He remained impervious to their glamour, invulnerable and strong in his own innocence, his vocation.

His vocation is of a lyrical rather than a speculative nature. And it was in a lyrical mood that he created those paintings of 1911 which were the most comprehensive expression of the mysterious processes which his psyche had undergone. Many of the works dating from the following two years are equally characteristic and significant – those in which he continues to be haunted by his past and his origins, but in a more direct way. Yet all these works are still in the same

74 Apollinaire, drawn by Chagall in 1911

75 *Adam and Eve*, study for *Homage to Apollinaire*

style, in the same Chagall manner, despite the many sources of spiritual unrest he encountered in the Paris he had so passionately longed for, and despite the bustling atmosphere seething with contradictions and with challenge that did not permit a moment's rest. So that his determination to find his own way is all the more admirable, and we find this aim expressed not only in the extraordinary poetic imagination of the masterpieces of 1911, but also in those less complex, almost realist works, which seem full of emphasis and are animated and brought into relief by compelling movement that amounts at times to a kind of frenzy. The artist is not impelled by any motive of theoretical research, nor is he confined or governed by any system – for him lyricism is all, and he pursues this lyricism with the utmost vigour, seeking to express it in its most vivid and passionate form.

118

What he found in Paris was thus not so much instruction as affirmation in himself together with the stimulus of a fertile, exhilarating atmosphere with its 'light of freedom'. To be free, that is to be oneself, is not something that can be learned, but it is possible to find the right physical and mental conditions, the right atmosphere and climate conducive to this expansion. The Paris, then, of this decisive period provided Chagall with this climate, but there was also the eternal Paris, 'my second Vitebsk' he was to call it, and the whole of France which he adopted as the true home of his art – not for what it could teach him, but for what it had to offer in its atmosphere as a place in which to stay, to feel alive and to create. Chagall found himself in harmony with the prodigious lyricism of the tumultuous Paris of the time. He also found himself in harmony with French

76 *Adam and Eve*, sketch for *Homage to Apollinaire*

culture as a whole, with its spirit, its history, its aims and its creations.

His awareness of this culture and especially of French painting was accompanied by a recognition of the nature of his own painting, more particularly of certain features to which he was devoting care and thought and which consequently became characteristic of his style. He has spoken of the 'light of freedom'. There is another term to be added to this, one with an equally poetic, if not mystical, sound: the colour of love. In associating these two terms, which frequently recur in his writings and are a part of his vocabulary, we feel ourselves drawing near to what makes up the fabric of Chagall's painting. Firstly there is nature, the natural element, space or preferably the sky, in which each form reigns supreme. And in all this, in the pleasing arrangement of these physical surroundings, there is such a strong and subtle outpouring of colour that it might almost be described as miraculous. This is what is meant by freedom-giving light and the colour of love, which Chagall uses as technical terms defining his way of painting. Let us adopt them for our own use, for we must admit there is no better way of describing Chagall's art, his style and his technique.

For this technique is not governed by rules and methods. It does not correspond to any school, nor to any of the splendid, glorious systems adopted throughout the history of painting, nor even to those being evolved at the time in the studios of Montparnasse and Montmartre. Chagall's genius lies outside every category and every aesthetic concept, and he was concerned less with defining his technique than with explaining the spirit behind it.

For this technique and the spirit of this technique are one and the same thing. Chagall does not illustrate his dreams or interpret them, and the colour of love is not a way of shading in love, it is colour itself, handled with love and itself endowed with all the powers associated with love. There is another word frequently used by Chagall which gives us some idea of the nature of this colour. The word is 'chemistry'. In his stumbling yet deliberate phrases, in language which achieves its most concise articulation through its very poverty,

Chagall is always talking of 'chemistry'. Chemistry, as he understands it, is the palpable mystery of colours, the weaving by use of colour of some kind of binding spell. It is a mystical term from the vocabulary of a religious man. But it also belongs to the vocabulary of an artisan, a worker who uses materials, mixing them on his palette, applying them to his canvas with strokes that may be light or determined, but always loving. Here we return to this word, for this operation, which is still a psychic operation, consists of tender attentions and intentions that make it into an act of love.

It is the colours that bring the canvas to life and give it its soul. In Chagall's painting they reach their full impact. The effect on the spectator comes entirely from the colours themselves and their relationship to each other, from the differences in light and shade, in transparency and density. Chagall's use of the word 'chemistry' to denote all this is most appropriate, for it is the name of an exact science that deals with the elements of which matter is composed, their varying combinations, their interactions and their possible mutations. He could have used alchemy in this context, which deals with the same phenomena but also has spiritual connotations. This would have led us to one of those dualist concepts which, in our search for the true Chagall, we have consistently tried to avoid and which are merely confusing platitudes. The chemistry of colours, not their alchemy, is the ideal which Chagall has chosen to pursue. Colours are concrete substances, but it is the genius of the man who handles them that determines the degree of harmony in their mutual attraction and repulsion, in their interdependence, in the drama they construct. It is his genius that gives colours their major effects and makes them combine to produce an image which must also include the element of love itself.

The artist has love in his soul and thus it appears in the finished work. Before it appears in its final form, however, the problem of its representation arises. This is the *technique* of which the artist speaks in his own technical terms, the one being light coupled with freedom, and the other colour inseparably linked with love. Love, however, is the spiritual state of the artist which provides direction for his technique. We have seen how in his work he rejects influences which are of no value to him, and how he remains aloof from the clamour of theoretical controversies despite his interest in them. Nevertheless, in all he produced in France – in the France where he found freedom, the complete freedom to paint and exist; where, in a word, he was given the chance to fulfil his vocation – he never ceased to familiarize himself with things he admired and with which he found himself in harmony. The whole world of painting enchanted him, and he would go to the Louvre to feast on it, but French painting in particular captured his enthusiasm on account of its indescribable 'freedom-light' and 'love-colour'. He has often stated his preferences. Naturally they lie outside the classifications of schools of painting – these things are meaningless for him. But the inspiration, or the spirit, is what moves him, the perfection of the supreme art of a particular artist, regardless of what school he may have belonged to or founded. It is hardly surprising that he admired Impressionism, this eminently French school, this invention of the French genius. It is not the theories of Impressionism, but the spirit and consequently the *chemistry* of Impressionism – its refinements, its restraint, its tact – and, in more concrete terms, the *technique* of Impressionism and the Impressionists that he admires, especially that of Claude Monet.

This preference will hardly come as a surprise. But it is significant for all that, as are all revelations of this nature. As a rule, however, one might expect an artist to be attracted by the work of another artist that either resembles or is in marked contrast to his own. This presupposes that one artist necessarily admires another because he is in the same tradition, or conversely because he finds this latter artist antipathetic, since he possesses what the former does not possess, and thus the artist feels it is right for him to profess admiration. Such notions are ridiculous in the extreme. For when an artist states his liking for another's work – for example, for a master from another age – this is a highly significant indication of profound affinities be-

77 *Profile at the Window*, 1919. Painted before Chagall moved to Moscow, this is one of the works that mark the beginning of his last Russian period

78 *A Gentleman*, 1920

tween the two, which, although not apparent at first sight, call for attentive study and much thought. In naming Claude Monet as one of his favourites, Chagall affords us a deep and significant insight into himself, his love of nature, his knowledge of the quality and composition of the elements, water, sky, vegetation, and into his sensitivity, to the changes in time and the seasons, and into his communications with the secret inner forces of nature whose activities effect changes of infinite and delightful subtlety.

We have seen that upon his return to Russia Chagall continued to be unaffected by theoretical controversies in art. These existed in the world of Russian art just as they did in Paris, and excited far-reaching interest. Futurism, constructivism, and all kinds of 'isms' were springing up which in some ways resembled the movements current in Paris, in others were quite different, for many of the leaders of the *avant-garde* in Russia were vital and original creative artists.

These movements also shared common features with parallel movements that were developing in Germany. But the only problems that disturbed Chagall were personal ones. His return to Russia had been a major event in his life. He felt a different man there, free and master of himself and his art, responsible in all matters, and it was as a different man that he applied himself to the great practical opportunities offered by the revolution. His experiments in theatre décor, too, with its problems of craftsmanship and technical skill, were of great importance. He also continued with his own work, and in all that he did wherever he was he remained impervious to public opinion and unconcerned by whether he was recognized as a Russian master or a Western master or whatever. But the heroic era of the revolution soon passed, Stalin was to begin his rule and settle all questions, including that of painting, in a manner that is now only too familiar.

Chagall, followed a few weeks later by Bella and little Ida, left Russia for good. He broke his journey in Berlin – an inflation-ridden, chaotic Berlin, a caravanserai of fugitives and lost souls, the scene of every kind of literary, artistic and social turmoil. Chagall could now judge for himself how much his work had gained in prestige in the artistic life of Germany since the time of his exhibition with the *Sturm* in 1914. Herwarth Walden, the frenetic moving force behind the *Sturm* movement, who turned it into a meeting place for Western and Eastern trends, had taken great pains to maintain Chagall's place in all this activity despite the hiatus of the war. However, he found difficulty in providing Chagall with a satisfactory account of his management of the artist's affairs, and this led to differences and unpleasantness between them.

Be that as it may, this was another instance where Chagall's art was in tune with one of the great artistic movements emerging at that time. German Expressionism was drawn to the violent and disturbed images in his work, with its pathetic and fantastic elements. It is easy to understand the interest artists like Max Ernst or Kurt Schwitters had in the revelation presented by Chagall's art.

All this makes us realize how much Chagall is a man of his time, immersed in his own period, pulsating with its aims and forces, yet without subscribing intellectually to any of its formulated theories. Chagall belongs to his time in the same way that he belongs to nature and to his own destiny. His destiny is indeed a part of the destiny of his time and inseparable from its tragic events. Moreover, all the intellectual and dramatic expressions of this period are in harmony with what Chagall himself was expressing.

At the time of his return to France in the autumn of 1923 this expression had reached its most perfect form. Chagall had completely fulfilled his vocation. He was himself. He was the painter he had to be. He was happy and was beginning to taste the fruits of glory. All the events in his career and all the experiences of his inner life had brought him to the point where he was able to continue his output of beautiful and rich work, and at the same time to apply himself to all the various opportunities that might arise to extend his field of endeavour. He was entering his period of maturity.

CHAPTER SIX

Chagall in France

From 1923 to 1941 Chagall's personal life and his work were to flourish. He spent his days in the land of his heart. The Paris to which he had returned was no longer as it had been before 1914 when the revolution in plastic techniques was taking place. Having previously led a life of poverty and struggle there, he now felt perfectly content and at home, at ease with its people and its surroundings. He was one of its citizens. Moreover, when the time came, he was to find it easy to acquire French nationality. At this time, however, he deepened his knowledge and his love not only of Paris, but of the whole of France. He chose different places in the country in which to stay and work: the Ile de Bréhat, Montchauvet near Mantes, Mourillon near Toulon, and Lake Chambon in the Auvergne. He felt a great affinity for the French countryside which has inspired so many painters.

The struggles for a new form of plastic expression in the world of art had abated and given way to joyful triumph. The new movement that now appeared on the scene was Surrealism and it could not fail to attract Chagall. Its programme was very much concerned with the 'supernatural' element that Apollinaire had detected in Chagall's painting, and it was Apollinaire, moreover, who was the first to use the word 'surrealism' when in June 1917 he called his *Mamelles de Tirésias* a 'surrealist drama', after having meant to say 'supernatural drama'. The meaning of the term 'surrealist' seems to have been rather vague and doubtless quite different from the one it was subsequently given by the young group who adopted it. In any case, it is clear that Chagall, who painted such strange pictures himself, was bound to find himself in sympathy with this movement. Sympathy yes, even complicity, but here as before there was no question of a theoretical commitment. Chagall has never been able to give his allegiance to any theory any more than he could oppose one. He is incapable of this kind of dialogue. We are familiar with the lively spirit of controversy that reigned among the surrealists; but try as they would, they never succeeded in drawing Chagall into the debate.

This outlook of theirs led them to lead a group life rather like a religious sect, and while it was no doubt a specifically intellectual enterprise it appeared to have a distinctly polemic flavour. And they canvassed for fresh recruits while debarring certain people from their ranks. It was only natural that they wanted Chagall to join them. But for him to make a decision of this nature was inconceivable. It was enough for him to pursue his own work along his particular road where he might chance upon companions making for similar goals. It was certainly reassuring for Chagall that on his return to Paris he should have found the forefront of activity taken up by a movement like Surrealism. Rebelling against the social order and the conventions of mechanical reasoning, it stood for everything that expressed or helped to express the freedom of the human spirit – dreams, chance, desire and revolt. There is an obvious affinity between Chagall and the spirit of Surrealism, and we can see how natural it was that he felt himself drawn to a poet like Paul Eluard, in the same way that he had fraternized with the poets of the Cubist period. The affection of these two noble and dedicated artists for each other has never abated – Eluard was to dedicate some beautiful poems to Chagall, and the latter was to illustrate many of them.

Chagall's fundamental preoccupation at this time more than ever before was his relationship to his art. Amidst the turmoil and upheaval he had lived through before returning to Paris, it had been impossible to salvage his works so that he now found himself, as it were, bereft of his points of reference. He had to make good the loss. He now repainted his early works either from photographs or from reproductions, making replicas of them or producing new versions. Between 1928 and 1929 he devoted all his time to this task. For him

79 *Chichikov's Arrival*. Plate I of Chagall's illustrations for Gogol's *Dead Souls*

it was a way of reviving his Russian memories and rediscovering their warmth and consolation.

But he was very soon presented with an opportunity of renewing his contacts with Russia in an even more positive manner. One of the results of this enterprise was to prove his ability in media other than painting, his ability to adapt himself to given conditions, and having accepted these, to master them. In short it proved him to be the universal master that a great artist very often is, and which Chagall became after his different apprenticeships and experiments, especially those dating from the years of the Russian revolution. As far as the graphic media are concerned, Chagall received his first instruction in Berlin in the studio of Hermann Struck, at the suggestion of

Cassirer, who had asked him for dry-point etchings and engravings to illustrate *Mein Leben*. At the same time he tried his hand at lithography and wood engraving. His mastery immediately established itself in the black linear strokes which, for all their simplicity, are paradoxically confident in their depiction of things and people, giving them depth, emphasis and movement. These are drawings of great character. Elsewhere he used a lighter stroke to make an interior alive with people and furniture, setting the whole into quivering motion. From then on Chagall was ardently committed to black-and-white art, able to execute it in all its variety. But the unifying link between these different techniques is his alert, spontaneous design, which, without sophistication, is remarkably direct and true.

This mastery is evident in the rich and varied engravings for *Dead Souls (Ill. 79)*. These 107 engravings were executed from 1923 to 1927. The eleven chapter headings were subsequently lost and remade in 1948 for Tériade's edition of the book. Dry-point engraving alternated or combined with etched engraving, and the artist also frequently used aquatint. In fact, all the processes were used to contribute to the throbbing, continually renewed and surprising graphic universe which is at the same time a human universe. At times the linear element predominates, supple, sharp and droll; elsewhere there is a slight haze, the black is softened and yet still forceful, with all the variety of expression of which the art of engraving is capable when handled by a great artist and great colourist. A medium as alive and free and with such infinite possibilities as this only remains to be translated into a space that is itself limitless, the kind of space that is natural to Chagall. One plate is completely filled with the trembling foliage of Pliushkin's old garden; on another, by contrast, the linear prevails over musical impressionism and we find ourselves in the presence of a great void, inside a circumference where tables and figures of men, or simply men's heads, are scattered about in a childlike manner without any regard for perspective – this is the contract office. And in passing in this way from plate to plate, from one diagonal to another, from one imperious gesture to another, from

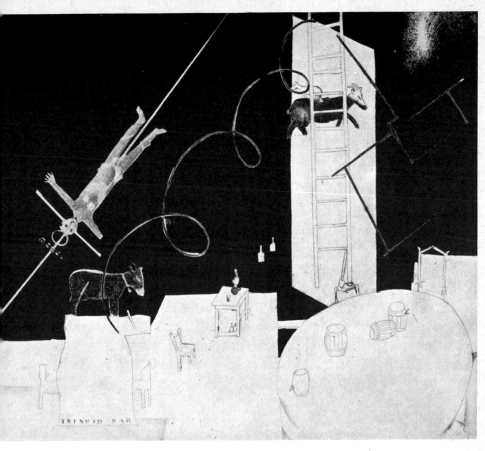

80 Scene design for Synge's *The Playboy of the Western World*, 1920

prominent corpulence to exaggerated curves, we find ourselves
transported from ordinary scenic space into a realm of mental space,
the realm of pure comedy. The art of black and white, far more than
colour, is appropriate for achieving this impression and making us
feel the essential nature of characters, of conversations, even of concrete objects, such as the houses in a town or foodstuffs.

In dealing with his stage settings for *The Inspector General* (*Ill. 61*),
I pointed out the affinity that existed between Chagall and Gogol.
It is most moving to see how this became manifest when Chagall,
having left a Russia that was about to sink into darkness, settled in

the freedom of France and found in Gogol his spiritual companion for the first four years.

Dead Souls, like *The Inspector General*, is the story of a deception. This is the kind of story certain to appeal to Chagall's sense of humour. In Moscow he had done the stage setting for Synge's *Playboy of the Western World* (*Ill. 80*). But the Russian version of this theme, as treated by Gogol, struck Chagall as the more incisive and stimulated his creative zest to the full. Chichikov had travelled through Russia performing a macabre but highly profitable confidence trick. By the light of this wonderful story we are plunged into the heart of the steppes, travelling its roads, stopping at its villages, inns and castles, entering the houses in the town, attending the Governor's ball, and meeting a host of larger-than-life characters, all of whom pale beside Sobakevitch, the bear-like landlord. We are the witnesses of a bewildering intricacy of bargainings and intrigue, swaggering and villainy. In short, it needed the machinations of a scoundrel to create this reality. That is to say this whole reality is founded on illusion and exists only through illusion, through the conjurer's magic wand, through the initiative of a producer, a man of the theatre. Russia exists only in terms of comedy.

Thus Chagall was to prove his comic genius equal to Gogol's. The speeches of the characters are completely without meaning, they talk for talk's sake. Yet this unreality is only apparent, so that we must still look for a meaning behind it, which might be stupidity or even spitefulness and deceit. Consequently the words convey a certain mood, and this is what the illustrator has to portray exactly, following the text step by step. Similarly, the faces of the characters and the appearance of the objects have to be exaggerated in the manner of a caricature. And yet, strictly speaking, we are not dealing with caricature. For caricature underlines a certain feature that is made to stand for vice, ugliness or the absurd in the character. But in this instance the character as a whole appears outrageous and exaggerated. The same is true of all the objects involved. For they too are prey to the demon of boastfulness and gossip, and seem bent on making their presence felt. Altogether it is not so much a matter of stressing the grotesque aspects of a certain kind of reality as of emphasizing the very existence of this reality. The world described here is not made farcical as a contrast to another, more serious world. It stands alone as farcical. It is buffoonery itself. And this is what makes it so atrocious and disorientating.

What do the scenes of *Dead Souls* have to tell? Nothing but the most ordinary occurrences, and it is just this that makes them so incredible. Such dullness and crudity, the way of eating and setting the table, the dishes eaten, the courtesies and compliments, the mediocrity of the scheming, of the drunkenness and the laziness – it is all exaggerated, it all unfolds like a dream. It is all fantastic, the work of a trickster, all simulated, all absurd; this Russia is a comedy. So that when the charlatan is unmasked everything disintegrates with him, and this Russia disappears into the steppes, borne off by the crazy careering of a bewitched troika.

But this, nevertheless, was Russia, and Russia is eternal. So we must go back to the beginning of the story and Chichikov must set off on his travels all over again, but this time he will be halted... Yet Russia will continue, dear as she is to the hearts of both the author and the illustrator, Russia, whose reality is more real than her unreality, whose humanity is more than the sad, paltry evidence of her humanity. Russia ... 'What future do those limitless spaces hold? You who are without end, are you the land of infinite Thought?'

This belief in a mystical Russia, with all its resources hidden in the limitless unrolling of its roads, in the perspectives of its destiny, in the dim soul and the unknown future deeds of its children, all this is deeply rooted in the heart of every Russian. In 1927 Chagall donated his ninety-six etchings for *Dead Souls* to the Tretyakov Museum in Moscow – 'with', as he wrote in his letter of tribute, 'all the love of a Russian painter for his homeland'.

He was now to enjoy complete freedom as a painter. He mastered all techniques and adapted them to his own purposes. The arbitrary way in which he divided up his canvases corresponded to his need to fill them: light-hearted fantasy, for example, is uppermost in pictures such as *Little Red Houses* (1924), *The Watering Trough* (1925) and *Peasant Life* (1925). In these pictures he portrayed the Russian countryside in a mood of perfect serenity. The painter now found unrivalled pleasure in looking at nature, at the sky and at Paris. This is the place to mention the window motif, so dear to Chagall, that he had already explored in 1909 in Vitebsk and again in 1915 at Zaolcha, with the view over the beautiful Slav forest, in a painting entitled *Window in Zaolcha*. There had also been a delightful canvas, *Paris through the Window* (*Ill. 36*), painted during his first stay in Paris in 1913. This again was full of the poetic eccentricities of the 1911 period, although with a lighter touch as if scattered by a capricious hand. The colouring suggests the vivid freshness on to which the windows of his second Parisian period were to open. The uprights of the windows were streaked with yellow, red, green and blue, like the window of a doll's house, a fairy ladder, some absurd multi-coloured toy. Lying on a chair near the window-sill was a huge, bushy bouquet of flowers that did not quite reach up to the window-sill and the view outside. A yellow cat with a human face sat on the sill. In the right-hand corner appeared a figure with two heads, one of them blue. The whole city was seen in outline, with a ghostly Eiffel Tower rising to the full height of the canvas. Like all the painters and poets of his time Chagall worshipped the Eiffel Tower. (He had also adored the ferris wheel, a left-over from the lavish world exhibitions, and had painted it – *The Ferris Wheel*, 1911–12 – before it disappeared for ever from the Paris skyline.) In *Paris through the Window* the Eiffel Tower rose high up in the painting while below, against the pale silhouette of the town, a man and a woman lay outstretched, side by side, tiny and black like insects. This no doubt was their way of taking a walk in the streets of Paris. But now we come to the first window paintings after Chagall's return to Paris, those in the Zumsteg collection, and above all *Ida at the Window* (1924, *Ill. 81*). Seated on the window-sill, all green

82 *Lovers under Lilies*, 1922–5

against a background of green, with a vase of flowers beside her, the graceful little girl turns her thoughtful profile towards the freshness of the scene outside. The colours are flooded with a kind of flower-like mood, the touch is infinitely discreet and delicate. Another charming window is the one in *Bride and Groom of the Eiffel Tower*

83 *Lovers with Flowers*, 1926. One of the large canvases painted at Mourillon

84 *The Open Window*, 1926. Painted at Chambon-sur-Lac

85 *Bride and Groom with Eiffel Tower*, 1928. The dominant motif here, as in
other pictures of the period, is the flower angel

(1928, *Ill. 85*). By contrast, here the mood is somewhat delirious
with an enormous splash of glowing colour, and once again a bouquet of flowers. Flowers are to appear in profusion throughout Chagall's work from this period onwards. The time spent in the Mediterranean light at Mourillon, where he worked on the gouaches commissioned by Vollard for the *Fables* of La Fontaine, prompted an
intoxicating profusion of flowers. Their colours grew stronger and
richer in the gouaches. He was now at the peak of his genius as a
colourist. His 'chemistry' had never been more skilful or more effective. But he was also at the peak of his happiness with Bella, and she
appeared to him daily amidst roses, arums and lilies.

The only works in the Bella cycle I have mentioned so far have been the sublime images painted at the time of their marriage, with the enchantment of kisses and figures spinning high up in the sky. When ecstatic joy is succeeded by a period of calm and perfect bliss, it is appropriate to consider the entire series of portraits, those works in which the painter does not abandon himself to a hymn of love, but catches the image of his beloved in every physical detail and puts all his heart into this task.

This gallery of masterpieces begins with *My Fiancée in Black Gloves (Ill. 5)* painted in 1909. We have seen how decisive were the early works produced in the years 1908 to 1909. Chagall's genius was instantaneous. At the outset of his career he was least inclined to delay. Complacency or a search for new effects may bring some artists to a temporary standstill. There is no such slackening of pace with Chagall, however; he has always maintained his powers of prompt reaction, upheld in this by his own healthy naïvety and his natural disposition. This disposition was at its most fertile when it expressed youth. He has succeeded in preserving youth like his child-hood, so that when this youthfulness is portrayed it has a statement to make and does so with trenchant clarity. It is this that shines out of the first portrait of Bella, which is a portrait of youth. Youth dwells in it, all sweetness and grace, all brightness, the clarity of black gloves against a black background. And the black gloves themselves, placed squarely on the hips with the fingers spread apart – what a curious idea, an idea that falls little short of effrontery, and yet what adorable effrontery! Added to this is the ruffled collar, sug-gesting children dressing up to act an Italian comedy.

There follows Bella as she appeared after the return to France. First there is a lithograph – *Bella in Profile* (1922–3), of which Moulot made fifty-six copies – and a *Self-portrait* which has an in-tense, princely beauty. *Bella in Profile* is moving because it is pos-sibly the best likeness that we have of her. Then there is *Bella with a Carnation (Ill. 86)*, a painting that dates from 1925. All traces of coquetry have now matured into a feeling of fulfilment and extreme

86 *Bella with a Carnation*, 1925. This large portrait has a 'classical' quality perhaps deriving from Chagall's work on new versions of earlier Russian pictures

sobriety. This is a supreme work that equals the most perfect portraits of the greatest periods, portraits that are completely dark and
unrelieved except for a touch of white in the linen or the face, those
famous portraits which in their nobility remain the illustration, *par
excellence*, of the human countenance. In comparing this portrait to
the works prized by museums, it might appear to be lifeless. But,
on the contrary, life surges through Bella's head, held slightly forward and tilted to one side, the eyes intent in their gaze and the lips
closed on words already spoken, the nostrils breathe, the whole face
is breathing, and it is as if the very subject of the picture were respiration. It is respiration itself that has been represented here: a living
being engaged in the act of breathing. The frail beauty of the slender,
pointed face is depicted here in the fullest expression of life.

In *Double Portrait* (*Ill. 87*) of the same year, 1925, Bella's face appears
in profile. This time the beloved is completely involved with life,
leaning forward to meet it in a posture that could easily lend itself
to aerial flight. She appears beside her companion, each of them
holding the emblems of their different roles in their hands, he with
his palette, and she with a bouquet of roses that contrasts with the
milky white of her dress. A delightful beret of the same white rests
on her hair. But are they in fact moving? She could be either seated
or suspended in air, and it is only her head turned in profile that
suggests an idea of motion. Her partner's profile is parallel to hers
and turned towards a picture frame which he supports with his
other hand and which is cut off by the edge of the canvas, a painting
which he has perhaps already completed or is about to paint, a mystery to come.

The two of them appear together again in *Lovers* (1928) tenderly
entwined amidst the foliage of some vague Eden. This time she is
dressed in black, with a large white collar. After the demon-
strative affection in this picture we return to a masterly example of
the portrait in the stricter sense, *Bella in Green* (1934, *Ill. 88*), with
the loveliest of greens, the bright lustre of the fan and the collar and
cuffs of lace standing out against it. There is the same spiritual ex-

87 (*right*) *Double Portrait*, 1924. Another large portrait linked stylistically with
the variants of works of the Russian period

pression on the face as there is in the portrait with the carnation, and the same seriousness, but the gaze is no longer straight ahead towards the outside world – now it is lost in the heights. It is this that produces a dream-like expression with perhaps a hint of sadness. In a study for this portrait, there is an angel to the left of the model whispering a secret into her ear. In the final version the angel has disappeared and the effect is improved; Bella is alone with her secret.

We must follow through this story of total adoration, of a perfect and harmonious love. Bella died in America on 2nd September 1944, just after she and her husband had heard the joyful news of the liberation of Paris which would have meant the end of their exile, and made it possible for them to return to the land they loved. We know that for Chagall, who was endowed with such vast reservoirs of emotion and who was so profoundly vulnerable, this tragic blow was overwhelming. When, after nine months of inactivity, he was able to return to painting, his first act was a final tribute to his late wife. He came across a large canvas dating from 1933 entitled *Circus People*. This was filled with all the usual figures and objects typical of Chagall's fabulous space: people in the air, an acrobat in tights, a figure in a Russian cap, a wedding, a fiddler, and high up in the painting a lamp and a samovar. The whole ensemble is dominated by a figure with an ox's head clutching an armful of foliage. In the bottom left-hand corner of the painting is the figure of a poet with his head upside-down and an open book in his hand, and almost in the middle is Bella with her fan and her demure dress, her delicate small head framed by black hair. In an oval-shaped inset between them Vitebsk appears as the image that unites them; they both think of it, without actually looking at it, although his head has come off possibly in an attempt to see it better. The extraordinary semicircular acrobat is pointing out their dear Vitebsk, rather like the page – or is it an angel? – unfolding the map of Toledo in the corner of one of El Greco's paintings.

With his heart deep in mourning, Chagall cut this canvas in two. The right-hand side later became *The Wedding Candles*. It was the

88 *Bella in Green*, 1934–5. The pathos and gravity of this portrait are almost biblical in character, and indeed Chagall was working on his Bible etchings at this time

other side that he now felt drawn to, and he immediately set to work, repainting it to produce *Around Her* (*Ill. 89*), the painting that has since become famous and is now in the Musée National d'Art Moderne in Paris. The figure in the bottom left-hand corner with its head upside-down has been filled in in greater detail and now holds a palette instead of the open book. The semicircle formed by the acrobat has been simplified and the oval enclosing Vitebsk, shining like an enormous bright moon in the darkness, now constitutes the focal point of this strange scene. Thus the elements are still the same as in the former great work, but there they had been intermingled with a whole disorganized accumulation of other elements; their impact had thus been diminished and their significance lost. In his grief the artist had taken them up once more, and in removing the superfluous details he had restored their dignity and pure form within this framework of nocturnal sobriety. Bella, too, was transformed, for she had just died, and this was the first image of a dead woman. She was mourned as every woman who dies should be mourned, but in this case no doubt the bereavement was so great that the living had no more tears to shed, so that here it is she who weeps. The dead woman weeps as she leans towards the vision of Vitebsk, Vitebsk with its houses beneath a sickle moon, riding through the bright sky within this oval, this great dew-drop, borne by the angel-acrobat. Bella personified Vitebsk: '... Basinka, Bellotchka from the mountains of Vitebsk, is reflected with the trees, the clouds and the houses, in the waters of the Dvina.' She had remained the embodiment of all the treasured memories of the beloved past throughout the course of this long union, which had found its permanent home in France. She had been conscious of all that she represented, for in the latter part of their American exile, as if aware that she would never return, she was in great haste to finish her book of childhood memories, and immediately to write its sequel. This second volume, like the first, was to be published in the original Yiddish under the title *The First Meeting*. It appears that she began this in 1935 after the journey to Poland, when the first intimations of

89 *Around Her*, 1945. Painted in spring 1945, after almost nine months' inactivity following Bella's death

the great persecution and the dreadful ordeals to follow were breaking upon the world.

Thus from their beginnings in Vitebsk and throughout all the times that followed she was to be Chagall's constant companion. The land of their origins was embodied in her presence, she was 'the Jewish fiancée'. 'Objects, people, landscapes, Jewish feast-days, flowers: these are her universe, and it is of these that she speaks.' 'She waits for me. Her whole being is listening for something in the same way that long ago, when she was still a little girl, she would strain her ears for the sounds of the forest.' 'I see her back and her delicate profile, she hardly moves. She is listening for something, she is thinking of something … and perhaps she can already see those worlds beyond …' Words like these appear in the harrowing preface that Chagall wrote for *The First Meeting*, the account of their first meeting and their love. In it he reveals his deepest secret. His memories had been formulated and given expression in his painting; they had thus become incarnate in the person of his loved and loving wife, in love daily shared. They had become the substance of life as he lived it, and the substance, too, of immortal painting.

Chagall had decided on a series of gouaches for the illustration of the *Fables* of La Fontaine commissioned by Vollard, intending to hand them over to a team of etchers who were to have executed them in black and white. Another commission from Vollard to illustrate circus scenes was also executed in a series of gouaches under the title *Cirque Vollard*. This cycle was accompanied by a series of paintings, likewise inspired by the circus, acrobats, equestriennes, and fairy-like figures covered in merging semicircular flecks. All the work of this enchanted period is ablaze with shimmering, lustrous, arbitrary flashes of colour, colour that emerges from areas of dark like the sparkle of precious stones or the flicker of flames. Here his cosmic 'chemistry' is at its most effervescent.

Offering Chagall the task of producing the illustrations of the circus and La Fontaine's fables had been an inspired move on the

90 *Donkey Cov-ered with Lion's Skin*, 1926. One of the gouaches for La Fontaine's *Fables*

part of Ambroise Vollard, although it is known that he was widely criticized for his choice. La Fontaine! The *Fables* of La Fontaine! To entrust this jewel of French genius to a barbarian from the East! Vollard remained unmoved, and he was right; works of universal culture belong to all the world, if not they would not be universal. Can the reading and the study, and consequently the illustration, of any national literature be restricted to the people of one nation? May Shakespeare only be acted in England and Molière only in France? Nationalist claims of this order can only lead to the most absurd stupidities. In the event, as Vollard pointed out, the fables which La Fontaine's genius had adapted in the seventeenth century

91 *The Clown with the Donkey*, 1927. One of the series of circus pictures Chagall painted while working on the illustrations for the *Fables*

originated from various Oriental traditions which were later assembled in Greek by Aesop, and subsequently taken up by others over the centuries in their own tongues. Now if there was one artist who seemed to have the ability to bring out the Oriental flavour of the original it was Chagall. Finally, surely there was a kind of pre-established harmony between the poetry of these fables, which is at once candid and malicious, and the art of a painter who, like Chagall, had such a love of plants, animals and nature as a whole?

In fact nothing could have lent itself more appropriately to the fantasy of Chagall than the *Fables* or the circus at a time when this fantasy was at its peak, expressing itself in a play of colours that was evidence of the highest attainment in this field. The atmosphere, the motifs and the animals of the *Fables* and of the circus have much in common, and with Chagall's impatient energy working on both together they fused into one and the same world, full of somersaults, leaping and running, of fur and feathers, of growls and watchful glances, awaiting the exact moment to jump on to a horse's back or to overpower the prey, a world of calculation and combat, of ruses, tricks and feats. It is a world of nature, a physical world in which bodies in their naked state, in their crude and animal condition, in their exposure to risks and dangers, are made to display their agility and their strength. At the same time this world of nature is a world of disguises and of comedy, boundless comedy which in the *Fables* is presented 'in a hundred different acts', and which in the circus arena unfolds with spectacular parades down below and in dizzy flights of stars soaring in all directions through the firmament of the 'Big Top'. Thus in its two-fold aspect this is a world of entertainment, a world of holiday-making. It is brimming with marvels, and the two stages present the same marvels, in particular the marvel of aerial flight. On the one hand there is the soaring of birds through the air, and on the other the exploits of trapeze artists in the ring. And it all ends in laughter. What we hear is the wisdom of the clown. The clown has the last word, for he draws the moral from whatever has just taken place. And what has happened? What have we been

A charlot Chaplin

Marc chagall 1929

92 *To Charlie Chaplin*, 1929

watching? The exploits of a juggler or a horsewoman? In his turn, the clown re-enacts these, and in so doing he demonstrates their inanity. Where strength is outwitted by cunning, or brutality triumphs over the weak and innocent, the clown tells us that this is right and as it should be.

It may be right, but it is still sad. Everything that happens is sad, but this cannot be changed. The clown knows this and moreover he knows that he, too, is doomed to a ridiculous and pitiful downfall, and that he like the others is a victim. He laughs, but in the knowledge that he is compelled to laugh. He is bound up with the implacable and ludicrous course of events in the world, he is the butt of all the world's misfortunes, of the petty, comic mishaps and the major catastrophes. He is a great philosopher, and this is his philosophy. It is the philosophy of that greatest genius among clowns, Charlie Chaplin, of whom Chagall did a superb drawing in 1929 (*Ill. 92*), in which the clown is walking with a wing under one arm.

This, then, is the philosophy of the *Fables* and the circus, and of those forerunners of Chaplin, Shakespeare's fools. For is there not something of the Shakespearean fool in Chagall? Is there not a strong element of Shakespearean clowning in his frequent coupling of an adorable feminine face with an ass's head or the head of a calf or a sheep, with Bottom's head? He himself expressly acknowledged this derivation when he painted his picture of *A Midsummer Night's Dream* (*Ill. 120*) in 1939, a magnificent painting lost in poetry. There is, however, a certain nuance here essential to Chagall's sentimentality. We may say that it is with only one part of Shakespeare and not with the whole that Chagall declares his intimate harmony, that side of Shakespeare which consoles us for Shakespeare as a whole, that side where he attempts to console himself for what he is. For the clown's philosophy is a cruel and bitter one, even where it is softened by Chaplin's fellowship of mankind. But it can be carefree too, and can redeem us by its fantastic elements and its aerial grace, the magic of Ariel. Thus it teaches us that in spite of the crushing yoke we may

93 *On the Sofa*, 1929. Painted in the Villa Montmorency, near Porte d'Auteuil, where Chagall painted many small pictures of nudes, brides, lovers and village scenes

have to bear we can yet discover hidden recesses of nature, of dreams and tenderness.

Chagall's enthusiasm is extended to all the animals of La Fontaine and the circus, and to all the animals of the enchanted night. He embraces them all, including those to which he had hitherto given little thought, and they all now find their place in the images of this period, in these striking gouaches each of which is an explosion of colour and clowning. His range of animals is unlimited. This becomes evident in his next paintings, amongst which is the huge flying fish in *Time is a River without Banks* (*Ill. 123*). New, too, is the cock. It first appears as the central motif of a painting in 1929 in *On the Rooster*. Here a charming creature is astride the rooster, her head lies tenderly along its beak, which is smiling blissfully.

Franz Meyer has compared one of the images of this period with *Alice in Wonderland*. This is a most apt comparison, and in no way an anti-climax after having mentioned Shakespeare. For the extravagance is the same in both, except that in Shakespeare it is a despairing black vision of passions, follies, kingdoms and destinies sinking together into the same inescapable abyss. With Lewis Carroll, however, such considerations do not arise since his writing remains at the level of childhood. Both these worlds find their place in Chagall's imagination, which feeds on memories and all the dimly-lit recesses of the subconscious. The fantasy world of both writers is equally child-like and depends upon accepting the most unlikely events without astonishment, and on regarding all members of the vegetable and animal kingdom as equals. It depends on speaking a droll, absurd, comical, inarticulate and incomprehensible language which belongs to a world other than the one in which we live and speak our own rational language. The language of this other world is the inconsequential language of Shakespeare's fools and jesters. It is the language of the nonsensical communication between Alice and the March Hare and the Cheshire Cat, and finally it is the language of Chagall, eternally capricious, with its unexpected juxtapositions, its hybrid couplings, its ass with the rooster's head.

94 *The Dream*, 1927. This painting belongs to Chagall's second circus cycle

At the end of 1928 Chagall set to work afresh on a new set of etchings for the *Fables* of La Fontaine, having been unable to use his original gouaches for this purpose. The new etchings, coming as they did after the *Dead Souls* and before the *Bible*, were among his master-pieces of graphic art. He exploited the medium to the full, in the way that his collaboration with Louis Fort and later with Maurice Potin had taught him. His gifts as a colourist, made manifest in the wonder-ful earlier gouaches, seemed to emerge in these etchings. Even in the black and white there is still a feeling of colour. Dry-point and aquatint have disappeared, gone is the linear style so often used in the *Dead Souls*. The hatching and cross-hatching, the layers of varnish, all the processes to which he resorts as a painter contribute to the

95 *The Satyr and the Wanderer*, 1927. One of Chagall's illustrations for the *Fables* of La Fontaine

96 *Fruits and Flowers*, 1929. Chagall produced many poetic still lifes in the years around 1930

97 *Nude over Vitebsk*, 1933

modulation of the greys and blacks, exploiting to the fullest their potential depth and richness. The animals of the comedy take on an imposing aspect, and the human beings that appear beside them are in their turn tinged with this mythical and Pan-like atmosphere that springs from the same roots as these wonderful ancient stories.

In the years from 1927 to 1930 Chagall returned to painting flowers and fruit. But there were also all the other themes of Chagall's key-board, with variations in every key, achieved with versatility, deli-cacy or force – memories of Russia, married couples and lovers, nudes, fiddlers, musical cows, vagabond clocks, not to mention a new cycle of circus paintings. The phantom of Vitebsk was to appear once again (*Ill. 97*), this time with a beautiful nude with black tresses

98 *Lovers in Moonlight*, 1926–8

99 *The Fiancée*,
1926

flying above it (*Nude over Vitebsk*, 1933). Elsewhere Vitebsk is seen
with the bridge over the Dvina behind the lovers' heads (*The White
Elderberry Tree*, 1930), and finally in another picture of 1930, *Lovers
in the Elderberry Tree*, the town is bathed in moonlight, whose magic
has called forth an enormous bouquet of pink, white and purple
flowers at the centre of which lie the lovers, tenderly embracing.
This same arrangement was to be expanded later in *Blue Air* (*Ill. 113*)
of 1938.

After living in the Avenue d'Orléans the Chagall family found a
peaceful, almost rural haven, first in Neuilly in the Allée des Pins,
where Lipchitz was their neighbour, and then in 1929 they moved

161

100 (*left*) *The Bridal Couple*, 1930. This and the picture on the right are two examples from 1930 of Chagall's preoccupation with the flowers-and-lovers theme

101 (*right*) *Flowers*, 1930

to the Villa Montmorency in the Allée des Sycomores near the Porte d'Auteuil. They were intensely happy in their various homes, and were visited by numerous friends, both old and new, artists, poets, writers – all people of the greatest human worth – amongst whom Jacques and Raïssa Maritain deserve special mention. Chagall also got to know more and more of the French countryside. There was one delightful trip in the company of Robert and Sonia Delaunay during which he discovered the Languedoc region as far as the Spanish frontier, made friends with Joseph Delteil in Limoux, and met Maillol once again in Collioure. Winter in the Savoie was no less entrancing for him. There followed the stay in Peyra-Cava, the journey to Palestine in 1931, to which we shall return later, the visit to Tossa del Mar, where he stayed in 1934, and the discovery of

163

102 *Church at Chambon*, 1926

103 *Return from the Synagogue*, 1925–7. This is one of the works that paved the way for the Bible cycle of the early 'thirties

Spain. An exhibition held in 1932 had given him the opportunity of discovering the Dutch museums. In the spring of 1935 he was invited to attend the opening of the Jewish Institute in Vilna, and this journey to Poland swept him back into the Judaism of his childhood. He stayed for a time at Villeneuve-lès-Avignon in the spring of 1937 before going to Florence and Tuscany, which made a deep impression on him. In between he saw much of the countryside and the villages of France, especially the Midi, which he was growing to love more and more. Receptive as he was to the whole world, curious about all its diverse aspects, enamoured with all forms of natural beauty and grateful for all the works of human genius of the past, Chagall was throughout this entire period like a man born for happiness and worthy in every way of all that he had received.

In the last ten years of this Parisian period Chagall worked on the gouaches and the etchings for his illustrations of the Bible, which was the outcome of his visit to Palestine in 1931. I shall examine this in a separate chapter devoted to Chagall as a religious painter. But this decade is rich in many other works which show an important change in the way he painted. The compositions now became larger and were more serious in mood. This was the period of the moving portrait of *Bella in Green* (*Ill. 88*), the *Circus People* – part of which, as we have seen, was to become *Around Her* (*Ill. 89*) – and the exuberant and tender poetic work, *Dedicated to my Wife*, completed in 1944. This, too, was the period of the *White Crucifixion* (*Ill. 112*), to which we shall also return in the chapter dealing with Chagall's religious works. The colour now lost its transparentness and became thicker and more vigorous. The reds, the salmon-pinks, the lemon, the rose, the blue and the green are all noticeably brighter, and yet they have a cooler tone. Masses and shapes now acquire more body and the figures move about in a larger dimension; the fantastic element has been given undeniable substance. The angels have become more effective, they have grown in strength and energy. With gilded wings beating, one of them hovers over the group of people dear to him in the artist's studio (*The Apparition of the Artist's Family*, 1933–6). *Angel with Palette* (1936) returns in a more expressive and realistic form to a similar figure, of which he had made a light and diffuse version ten years earlier. As for the flamboyant angel (*Falling Angel*, 1933–47, *Ill. 119*) that swoops through all the phantasms common to Chagall's world, but that is here suddenly plunged into terrifying night, it is difficult to know exactly what to make of this, and whether the significance lies in the traditional chastisement associated with the rebel angels. But the striking thing here, as in the majority of the works of this period, is the decisive vigour in the composition of the images, a kind of monumental prominence in the figures. Other outstanding

104 (*right*) *The Cellist*, 1939. Chagall's mood of elation in the late 'thirties found expression once again in a cycle of circus pictures, of which this is one of the most important

examples of this grand manner are *Bride and Groom of the Eiffel Tower* (1938–9), *The Blue Donkey*, *Musical Clown* and *Mother and Child*. There is also the strange *Cellist* (1939, *Ill. 104*), with full face and profile both issuing out of one head, which is singularly inexpressive despite this duplication, and consequently all the more disturbing. The cello that forms the musician's body fills the whole picture, standing out against a snow-covered town bathed in cold, blue moonlight, while at the feet of this fabulous giant a tiny calf, clothed in blue, lifts up his gentle snout and seeks to follow the lead of the cello's melody on his own miniature violin.

105 *Snow-covered Church*, 1928–9. Painted in Savoy, during Chagall's first winter in the Alps

CHAPTER SEVEN

Chagall and World Events

World events during the 'thirties must be recognized as one of the
influences responsible for the enlargement and dramatization evident
in the art of Chagall. The threat of fascism and Nazism was spreading
throughout the world. In 1936 the Chagalls moved house once again
to the Villa Eugène Manuel near the Trocadéro. This was the year of
the Popular Front and the Spanish Civil War, and through the circle
of friends that came to visit them the Chagalls knew and shared in
the passion that was currently dominating French intellectual life.
Chagall could not remain insensitive to this mood. Descended from
the race of the prophets, he had by nature as well as by personal experience a feeling for both collective and personal destiny. He knew
that nothing under the sun is secure, that all is impermanence and
adventure, and that this impermanence and adventure is the common
destiny of all mankind.

In a century so full of disturbances, shocks were inescapable. Chagall had already experienced his share of them to a large degree.
During these years of anguish, when catastrophe was imminent and
people felt themselves on the threshold of fresh wars and revolutions,
Chagall could not forget that he had already experienced a war and
a revolution in which he had participated to the full. Now it looked
as if this were about to happen all over again. His memories of this
experience were always with him, and it had become an obsession.
Chagall's consciousness was constantly filled with the threat of a
virtual apocalypse.

The strange, large picture painted in 1933 and entitled *Revolution*
is evidence of this preoccupation. 'Revolution' was a word that
resounded ceaselessly in the mind of Chagall. Having once lived

106 Study for the *Revolution*, 1937. The political uprising represented on the

through a revolution, for him the echo of the word grew louder as the temporary calm of the intervening years gave way to a renewed onslaught in the quest for justice. It is this echo that we should listen for in this painting, rather than seek to decipher all its motifs and its general meaning. For this is the echo of an explosion at the centre of all these motifs, and at the centre of the painter's inner world.

left of the canvas is balanced by the artistic and human revolution on the right

Nothing has changed within this inner world – the unchanging motifs of yesterday, today and tomorrow are still there, unshaken and unaltered, yet co-existing quite naturally with this explosion. The man whose inner world this is remains undeterred by this explosion; he is still the same person, the same poetic dreamer, the same tender, loving, generous person he has always been. He cannot be expected to change intellectually with the advent of this explosion. He is no dogmatist, no politician; he cannot mould his actions to suit some theory and still remain true to his own inner world. Yet he voluntarily and quite deliberately entitles one of his paintings *Revolution*.

Where is the revolution, the explosion in this painting? Firstly, in the red flags to the left, and in all the armed men on the march, the masses of people pressing forward and shouting behind the oblique ramp separating them from the platform. In the centre, legs in the air, an upside-down figure balances on one hand on a table with the other hand stretched out sideways. His face is visible: it is Lenin. The rest of the scene is filled with motifs that are already familiar to us: the donkey seated on a chair, the samovar, the ladder, the open book, the bride, the painter surrounded by his musicians and his animals, the tramp with his sack, a corpse in the snow, a pair of lovers on the roof of a wooden house. Clasping a scroll of the Torah to his body, an old Jew sits meditating at the table on which Lenin is performing his acrobatics.

In 1943 Chagall was to cut this enormous canvas into three parts. Two of these were later re-named *Resistance* (1948) and *Liberation* (1952, *Ill. 107*), also highly evocative titles. It is interesting to see that the titles later given to the individual pictures were implicit in the original *Revolution*. But the paintings themselves, which the artist intended to express his emotion at the events he witnessed, are of little significance. Our interest in them is restricted to interpreting and explaining them – it is the emotion behind them that moves us and communicates itself to us, and it was this emotion that the artist was anxious to record. In its reference to the event, the image does not communicate any clear message that could be formulated in political terms, even of the most sentimental nature. There is no communication inherent in these images, they are simply a record. We are familiar with the curious symbols and motifs of Chagall's inner world, and he adds nothing conceptual or doctrinal, no declaration or proclamation, no cry of alarm or shout of enthusiasm to the representation of this inner world; it remains consistent,

unaltered and true to its own tradition. Yet it can produce works with such titles as *Revolution, Resistance* or *Liberation* rather like a piece of music whose title is evidence of some composer's dream of the deliverance of his native Poland, or of another's disillusionment at witnessing the degradation of the ideal behind the French Revolution, causing him to weep *sulla morte di un eroe*. Musical idiom, varying with the personal vocabulary of the individual composer, has the mystical faculty of linking a page written in this idiom with an event that has profoundly affected its composer. Similarly, Chagall the artist felt a passionate need to link certain pictures painted in his own, highly individual idiom to three events that for him, for his destiny and for his entire human existence were major events, the great tragedies of his century.

During this time of growing menace Chagall was working on his illustrations for the Bible. Throughout this whole period he was completely immersed in the history of his people, a history of trials, prophecies and disasters. The feeling of belonging to a history that was continually and eternally unfolding was strengthened by his visit to Poland in the spring of 1935, having been invited to attend the inauguration of the Jewish Institute in Vilna. Here he rediscovered the scenes and the atmosphere of his native Vitebsk. While in Vilna he had painted its synagogues, sensing that these, together with this whole way of life from which he himself had grown both physically and spiritually remote, were in mortal danger of extinction. He had met Dubnov, the Jewish historian and scholar, in Vilna and had seen his son mocked and beaten in the street.

Meanwhile war had broken out. After spending some months in Saint-Dyé, a village on the Loire, the Chagalls moved further south to the ancient village of Gordes in Haute Provence. It had been discovered by André Lhote, and was subsequently to become a favourite of many artists. This was to be the Chagalls' last home in a France that was now heading for disaster. Chagall worked furiously, painting still-lifes of fruit and flowers, and portraying himself in his work either as an angel or as the artist crucified.

108 *The Yoke*, 1930

109 *White Lilacs*, 1930

110 (*right*) *Mother*, 1935. Like *The Cellist* (Ill. 104), the imaginative articulation and vivacity of this canvas can be attributed in large part to the more relaxed and happy atmosphere in which Chagall worked during the middle and late 'thirties

He completed works that he had started earlier, such as the extraordinary *Red Cock* (*Ill. 111*) – rushing, huge and frightening, towards a thick bush in which there are several figures – and another outstanding painting, *The Three Candles* (*Ill. 114*), where again we find the magical mass of foliage, this time full of white roses. Here the pair of lovers have not found their customary haven, as in *Blue Air* (*Ill. 113*) and so many other happy pictures, but are perched on a carmine cloud out of reach of the refuge below them, above the village and the various figures beneath that are dominated by the three immense, vertical candles. They float, leaning obliquely as if clinging to one another in an apprehensive embrace. Pressed against each other in this movement of retreat, they gaze at the three strange, silent, funerary, eternal flames.

111 (*left*) *The Red Cock*, 1940. Completed while Chagall was living in the village of Gordes in Provence, after the outbreak of war

112 (*above*) *White Crucifixion*, 1938. This large composition is one of the major works of the 'thirties. The scenes around the Cross, in Franz Meyer's words, 'constitute an exemplary Jewish martyrology'

113 *Blue Air*, 1938

114 *The Three Candles*, 1938–40

115 *Homage to the Past*, 1944

It is impossible to remain unmoved by this evolution in the portrayal of the motif of the lovers, with its premonition of world-
wide disaster and personal mourning. The same feeling overtakes us
as we look at another representation of a couple in *Between Darkness
and Light* (*Ill. 116*). This painting was probably first conceived in 1938,
developed further during this later period, and given its definitive form
in America in 1943. Here the couple stands out against a sinister
winter's night, populated with several phantom apparitions – the

116 (*right*) *Between Darkness and Light*, 1944

sleigh, the lantern-man, the woman with a bird's head crouching in a corner with her child. Never has the couple presented such a picture of confusion. He is a solid shadow in greenish-black, holding his palette in one hand; she has a profile of deathly white joined to the front view of her face, with an extra eye, nose and even an extra mouth. This head in profile seems to be attached to some vague red scarf. A white form appears to indicate her dress and body, but its outline seems like a frame against the edge of the canvas itself – possibly this is a portrait of Bella leaning out of the canvas in order to throw herself into the arms of her artist, to bury her face in his.

Marc Chagall

117 (*left*) *Christmas*, 1943. Pen drawing for *Vogue* magazine

118 (*right*) *Bonjour Paris*, 1939–42. Begun in France, this was completed three years later in America

119 *The Falling Angel*, 1923–33–47. This work has a more fluent rhythm than the two earlier versions, and the motifs of the crucified Christ and the mother and child have been added to the 1933 version

In so far as this was still possible, the Varian Fry Committee and the American Consul General in Marseilles had succeeded in rescuing a number of intellectuals and artists who had fled to the southern area. After the fall of France they urged Chagall to leave immediately with his family. When several incidents had demonstrated the increasing gravity of the situation, Chagall finally agreed with great reluctance. He and Bella left Marseilles and reached Lisbon, while Ida and some friends saw to the assembly and dispatch of all his works, including the paintings in his studio. On 23rd June, the day that the U.S.S.R. entered the war, Chagall and Bella arrived in New York.

120 *Midsummer Night's Dream*, 1939. Although the lovers in this picture presumably represent Bottom and Titania, the animal-headed man is a familiar Chagall motif dating back to 1911

121 *The Gree Eye*, 1944. Th is another Cha gall 'fragmen cut from a large picture (painte c. 1926)

After the pre-war years when pathos had been the dominant mood in his work, there followed his American period with its renewed output of crucifixions and pictures showing flames and fire. Two pictures immediately loom large. In *War* (1943, *Ill. 122*) the memories of former days return in an imposing and haunted guise, and the wooden houses and the cow appear again in *Green Eye* (1944, *Ill. 121*). Apparently this strange composition harks back to a very early sketch Chagall did for a shop sign for a dairy. During this American period Chagall also returned to earlier canvases and worked them over or cut them up, turning them into several new works. All this work was in a highly expressive, indeed fantastic style.

122 (*right*) *War*, 194

123 (*above*) *Time is a River without Banks*, 1939. Related in the use of colour to both *The Cellist* (*Ill.* 104) and *Midsummer Night's Dream* (*Ill.* 120)

124 (*right*) *Vase of Flowers, At Night*, 1943

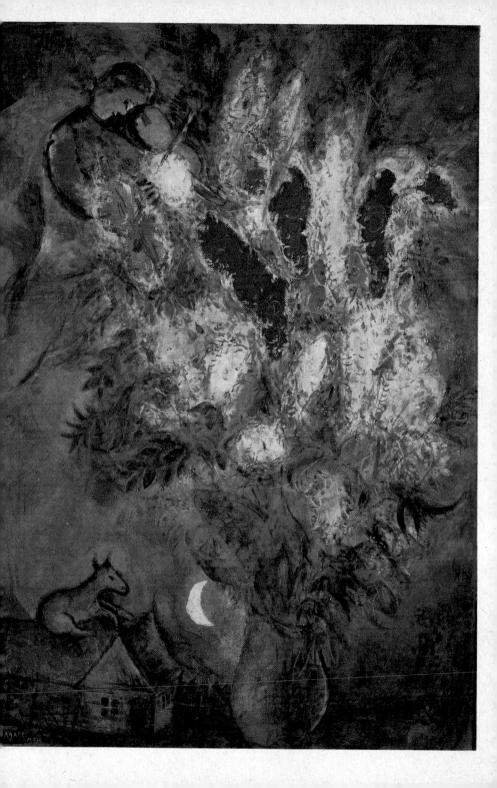

125 *Wedding*, 1944.

126 *Horse and Child*, 1944

We have seen that this period produced important works like *To my Wife*, the first version of which was painted in 1933. In this time of exile Chagall reviewed his whole universe, taking stock as it were. He returned to the circus people and to his animals, especially to the latter – the donkey, the cock, the hen with flowering plumage, the red horse, the dreaming horse and the goat appeared repeatedly. The pathetic and fantastic elements reach their culmination in *Wedding* (1944, *Ill. 125*), with its zones of colour independent of the shapes, relating to spiritual regions rather than to places and people. A vague red canopy virtually cuts the picture in two, with the sombre tones of wedding below contrasting with the brilliance of the musical angels above, a division that inevitably recalls certain visionary compositions by El Greco. Equally fantastic is another picture from the same year entitled *Listening to the Cock* (*Ill. 128*), but here the forms have been reduced to mere symbols, symbols that are difficult to read (for example, the blue head of the cock and the

127 (*left*) *The Sleeping Guitar*, 1943. One of a series of gouaches executed by Chagall during his visit to Mexico

128 (*right*) *Listening to the Cock*, 1944

yellow crescent moon that has fallen from its firmament into a chance position). All these symbols, moreover, appear in haphazard confusion, nothing is in its place, all is arbitrary. This is doubtless one of the most poetic pages ever written by Chagall.

Chagall was affectionately welcomed by his friends at the Museum of Modern Art and by American artistic circles – James Johnson Sweeney in particular – and he was happy in the company of his fellow emigrants from France. He did not remain in New York all the time, but often worked in the countryside, where he found the companionship of the nature so dear to him. He did not learn English, speaking Yiddish whenever the opportunity arose, in the every-

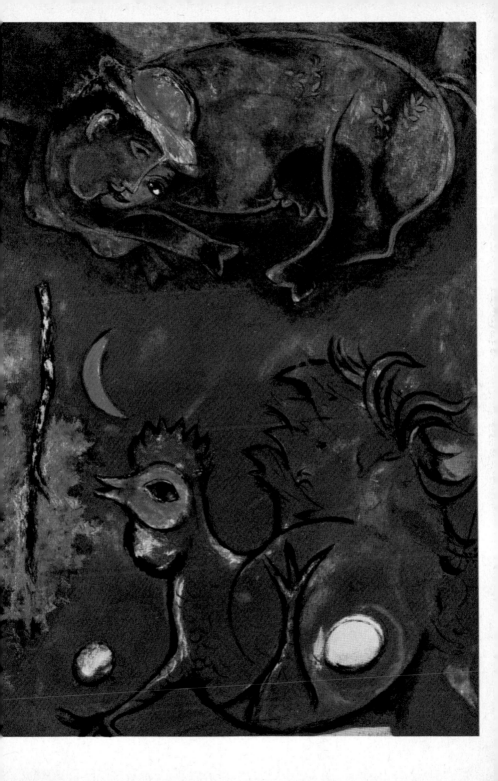

day encounters with Jews on the street, in shops and with newspaper vendors. Now that Russia had entered the war and found herself deeply involved in world events, Chagall's ties with Russia were renewed and he became more than ever aware of them. Upon his arrival in the United States he had been requested to design the settings and costumes for the ballet *Aleko* which a New York company, The Ballet Theatre, intended to perform in Mexico. *Aleko* is a ballet with music by Tchaikovsky, based on a poem by Pushkin. Leonide Massine was the producer, and for several months Chagall worked in daily collaboration with this distinguished choreographer. Surrounded thus by the world of Massine, Tchaikovsky and Pushkin, Chagall found himself back in Russia. He also made a point of meeting the Russians in the cultural mission sent by the Soviets to their American allies. Through them his grief-stricken heart felt in contact with Russia at war.

The ballet gave him the opportunity of getting to know Mexico, or at least of forming an impression of it, and this was an enormous source of pleasure to him. Judging by the few gouaches he brought back, he must have been profoundly impressed. They show how Chagall's genius instantly divined the Indian soul, sensing all its truly primitive aspects stemming from the Indians' familiarity with the forces of nature, with animals and with death.

After the death of Bella, Chagall painted several companion pictures to *Around Her* and *Wedding Candles* which, like these works, bear the imprint of a grief sharpened by the sombre memory of the recent years of war and exile. These are dark pictures relieved only by a few bursts of colour or light like the white, fantastic veil of the bride that snakes up behind the painter in *Soul of the Town*, or the red of the peasant woman, the gold of the cockerel's head and the streaks and touches of green in its plumage in *The Flying Sleigh* (1945, *Ill. 131*). The grief grew more intense, displaying the ultimate extremes of melancholy in *Self-portrait with Wall Clock* (1946) and *Nocturne* (1947, *Ill. 133*). This was grief of an unusual kind; far from making the artist withdraw into himself, it stimulated his imagina-

129 *Autumn Village*, 1939–45

130 *Obsession*, 1943. Based on sketches that Chagall had done in Europe, this painting links the theme of suffering with war motifs. And, like the *White Crucifixion* (*Ill.* 112), it is dominated by flame colours

tion and inspired the strangest scenes hitherto found in the work of Chagall. The element of the fantastic here is in no way gratuitous, capricious or purely extravagant, nor is it a departure into the realms of insanity or fear. Moreover, it does not take the form of buffoonery as elsewhere in Chagall's works. It is none of these things, and yet how is one to define this fantastic element? It is like a curious narrative outpouring of grief, where one might have expected to find the dumbness of inward-turning sorrow. Thus we find ourselves faced with the question of whether these paintings of Chagall's are examples of a fantastic interpretation of grief, or whether they depict the sorrowful aspect of the fantastic. In either case they present a fresh and vastly disturbing realm to our sensibilities.

131 *The Flying Sleigh*, 1945. The motif here recalls the earlier *War* (*Ill.* 121), but the prevailing mood of gloom is relieved somewhat by the natural liveliness of the rendering

132 *Self-portrait*, 1947

133 *Nocturne*, 1947

134 *Green Night*, 1948

During the summer of 1945 Chagall found various retreats in the
American countryside, finally settling in Sag Harbour while he
worked on a new commission from the Ballet Theatre for the curtain, scenery and costumes for Stravinsky's *Firebird*. Once again he
found himself thrust into the heart of things Russian, here in their
most Oriental incandescence, in the dazzling guise of a magic, fairy-
tale world.

135 *The Blue Violinist*, 1947

136 *Winter Sky*, 1942–50. At once folk song and fantasy, this painting falls within the context of Chagall's American work rather than that of his return to France

Chagall was now bent on returning to Paris. He made two trips to Paris, the first of which in May 1946 filled him with understandable emotion. Franz Meyer attaches great importance to the gouache and pastel sketches done at this time. The range of réséda and mauve, green and violet against a background of black creates a new mood, and became the starting point of the later 'Paris series'.

Chagall returned to France for good in August 1948. During his second trip to Paris at the end of the previous year a retrospective

137 *The Black Glove*, 1948

138 Drawing for *Four Tales from the Arabian Nights*, 1948

exhibition of his work had been held to inaugurate the newly established Musée National d'Art Moderne. Other European capitals or-
ganized their own Chagall retrospective exhibitions – at the Stedelijk
Museum in Amsterdam, at the Tate Gallery in London, at the Kunst-
haus in Zürich, and at the Kunsthalle in Berne. At the Venice Bien-
nale of 1948 an entire room in the French Pavilion was given over
to Chagall, and he was awarded the major prize for graphic art.

   True to his love of the countryside, Chagall moved initially to
Orgeval, near Saint-Germain-en-Laye, a region dear to the Impressionists. It was bathed in the Impressionist light, which he was happy
to rediscover. But the southern light was just as essential for him.
He made a trip to Saint-Jean-Cap-Ferrat, and then settled for good
in Vence. This whole stretch of coast had become a sort of Tuscany.

139 *Fishes at Saint-Jean*, 1949. One of the gouaches Chagall painted at Saint-Jean in the spring of 1949

140 *The Sofa,*
1950

Since the time of Renoir and Bonnard the most brilliant geniuses of modern painting have been coming to settle here in their years of maturity. It is a glorious place, and inevitably it has become fashionable. Yet all the great artists and poets who have settled there have succeeded in perfecting their work and fulfilling themselves, and have created an atmosphere of blissful solitude, communing only with the beauty of the landscape and the workers in the vineyards.

Thus while Chagall was living at his house, 'Les Collines', in one of the most beautiful regions in the world, all the painting he produced bore the splendour and the blue of the Mediterranean. Meanwhile in Tériade he had found a worthy successor to Vollard for handling his graphic works. It was Tériade who finally published *Dead Souls*, the *Fables of La Fontaine* and the *Bible*, the three great

141 *Mauve Nude with Two Heads*, 1950

142 *The Goat*

volumes originally commissioned by Vollard. On his own initiative
Tériade now commissioned Chagall to illustrate *Daphnis and Chloe*.
The first gouaches for this grand project took shape at Saint-Jean-
Cap-Ferrat. Nothing could have been better suited to Chagall's pas-
sion for the Mediterranean, and for ancient and pagan Greece.

This was a period in which Chagall's art came into full bloom. He
completed pictures he had begun in America and started on new
ones, and in all of them we can see the formulation of a broad,
powerful style that needs a large format to accommodate it. The
canvas is covered with bold forms, often in diagonals and in colouring that is strikingly intense, as in *The Red Sun* (1949) or *Blue Circus*
(1950, *Ill. 143*). But possibly the supreme example of the spectacular

143 *Blue Circus*, 1950

144 *Vence: Night*, 1952–6. All the shapes in this work grow out of nebulous, interlocking zones of red and blue

brilliance achieved by Chagall during this period, at the zenith of his art, is one of the Saint-Jean-Cap-Ferrat gouaches, *Fishes at Saint-Jean (Ill. 139)*. This is a fascinating and overwhelming painting, saturated with blue – sky blue and navy blue, against which there is an explosion of yellow – in a combination of sun, moon and flowers. The depths of this nocturne have been pierced by a magician's hand. Their bodies cut short by the horizon, the dreamy faces of the two lovers rise up between the sea and the sky.

The few gouaches done in 1951 at Drammont, a small resort near Saint-Raphaël, are in quite a different mood. Here the two elements of sea and sky seem to take on an ominous quality. The boat or the fish have the same carefree appearance as in other works, but the

145 *(right) Bouquet at Saint-Jean*, 1949

general atmosphere is a sombre one. It is like a return to tragic thoughts, and emerges most strikingly in two works from the same period, *Lovers at the Stake* and *The Cock on the Shore*.

The French Riviera is not only the home of the best artists of our time, it has also become one vast workshop, a centre of craftsmanship. There are certain buildings that will preserve the memory of the geniuses that live in this region. But the artists have also made their mark in the rebirth of certain crafts, which is a phenomenon of great importance not only because it emphasizes the vitality of these crafts, but because of the interest shown in them by the leading creative artists in modern painting. It is an example of the universal approach of these artists which the great masters of past ages strove for and achieved.

147 (right) Black Pitcher, 1955. This and the dish opposite are two outstanding examples of Chagall's ceramic work

Chagall now became eager to teach himself to make ceramics and to learn about firing processes. This is a flourishing industry in Vallauris and in his own immediate district, and we are familiar with the wonderful productions of the Madoura studios. At this time Chagall also turned to sculpture in stone. But both these techniques presented a problem, the problem common to every painter who tries to transpose his art into dimensional space: instead of adapting his technique of painting to the new material, the painter must evolve a new technique from this material, material which changes under his eyes and under his hand, and as the work progresses he must be able to allow for the nature of the material and anticipate its contingencies and its demands.

215

146 (left) Red Dish

148 *Boy and Dervish*. A Chagall lithograph for the illustration of the *Arabian Nights*

Chagall's sculptures have a confident grace, but it is in ceramics, a medium where colour reigns supreme, that he has been especially able to find scope for experiment and fulfilment. He has produced works in this medium – plates, vases and wall plaques – that are delightful in their brilliance. It was during this same period that he developed a passionate interest in lithography, working in black and in colours. He had already tried his hand at the latter while in America, with his *Arabian Nights* (*Ill. 148*), the illustration of forty tales from the *Thousand and One Nights*, commissioned by Jacques Schiffrin for Pantheon Books. These lithographs are without any doubt one of

149 (*right*) *Green Landscape*, 1949. One of the Saint-Jean gouaches

150 *Quai de la Tournelle*, 1953

the most dazzling portrayals of the treasures and the mysteries of the Orient. Back in France, Chagall was given the use of Fernand Mourlot's workshops, where he pursued this medium both in black and in colours, triumphing in both. His work in this field has a strong and lively quality. Many of his colour lithographs were published in issues of Tériade's *Verve*, and in *Derrière le Miroir*, Aimé Maeght's publication.

In July 1952 Chagall married Valentine Brodsky (Vava), whose gentle, radiant charm and wise and upright nature were to exercise the most favourable influence on this tormented soul. He had had a

151 *Portrait of Vava*, 1953–6. Here the flowers are a source of light that illuminates the entire picture

152 *The Panthéon*, 1953. A painting from Chagall's Paris series

wide experience of joy and pain and had lived through the most
extraordinary and often the most terrible world upheavals. Now
at last he was a ship entering harbour. At this moment of glory and
happiness he felt impelled to sum up, to express his heartfelt grati-
tude. This he did in the cycle of his Paris pictures, which were subsequently shown in a magnificent exhibition at the Maeght gallery
in June 1954. The series consists of some thirty large pictures, plus a
considerable number of sketches and small versions of the pictures
and several lithographs. Chagall's whole heart and mind were involved in this theme. He projected his passionate love of Vitebsk
on to Paris. He was fully aware of doing so, for he knew that he

153 *The Carrousel of the Louvre*, 1953–6. In this, another of the Paris series,
Chagall has encircled the Three Graces from the Triumphal Arch of the Carrousel and placed then beside the Eiffel Tower

154 *Bouquet and Red Circus,* 1960

155 *The Creation of Man*, 1956–8. In this work, based on a 1934 etching, the Elysian blue of the lower half contrasts with the bright, warm colours of the upper half in which Adam, David, Moses, a prophet, an angel and others encircle the whirling sun

needed to be possessed by this kind of love for a place; this sanctification of a place was necessary to him, he needed his holy city. From now on it was to be Paris, although this in no way prevented Vitebsk from pursuing its own privileged existence within him. Indeed, a Russian village in the snow appears in one of his Paris pictures.

223

156 (left) *Sunflowers*, 1955

157 (right) *The Opéra*, 1953.
Another painting from the
Paris series

Moreover, all the recurrent motifs of his whole life reappear in these pictures. They now march through the vast expanse of Paris, divided by the Seine with its bridges. And the monuments of Paris are themselves motifs in the life of Chagall, just as much as the donkey, the cock and the lovers. Here as everywhere there is the eternal couple. The sun and the moon, the nights and the seasons

158 *Clown with Violin*, 1956

159 *The Red Jacket*, 1961

follow each other in interminable succession – or, strictly speaking, intermingle – throughout Chagall's work in defiance of all the laws of nature.

This universe of Chagall's is at the same time real and unreal, factual and imaginary. Nothing there is ever permanent, everything immediately becomes endowed with a spiritual form. Nothing ever takes place in it without being transformed into an obsessive memory or a fervent passion. This is the universe of Chagall's destiny, the universe in which his destiny does not unfold, but is deliberately fashioned. His destiny forms itself into a universe where all its qualities of time and space take on a concrete form. Everything is here –

160 *Equestrienne,*
1955

things, events, fortune and adversity, emotions and dreams, pres-
ences and absences are simultaneously evident in a perpetually fluid
arrangement, in a double paradox of time and space, for time is a
river without banks, and so is space.

This universe of Chagall's destiny is also his artistic universe, the
world of his pictures. It, too, is without banks; vague and infinite,
it embraces every possible form and is lit with all the colours of the

161 *Acrobat*, 1955

prism. Chagall's colouring appears to have attained its most dazzling quality in this Paris series. The waves of colour that surge over these large areas, unconfined by outlines, set the whole firmament of Chagall's universe shimmering, and night and darkness merge without in any way detracting from the overall brilliance.

The paintings that followed this great Parisian spectacle included a return to the themes of the circus and of flowers, and all display the

162 *The Flute Player*, 1954. This colourful and moving pastorale was painted at Olympia during Chagall's second visit to Greece with Vava

163 *The Green Cock,*
1956

same chromatic richness and the same freedom. Chagall is master of his
orbis pictus and arranges it with delight. The greatest source of pleasure
in this period, however, was his two journeys to Greece in the company of Vava, the first immediately after their marriage (*Ills 164,
165*), and the second two years later in the autumn of 1954 (*Ill. 162*),
when he went to prepare the illustrations for *Daphnis and Chloe.*

164 *Boat with Two Fishes*, 1952

As was usually the case in projects of this nature, the lithographs were preceded by a series of gouaches. These encounters with the world of Greek mythology made a strong impression on Chagall. The shock of initial impact was succeeded by a perfect harmony.

232

165 *The Sun at Poros*, 1952. Painted during Chagall's first visit to Greece with Vava

168 *Paris Opéra Ceiling*, 1964. This monumental work was unveiled in autumn 1964, after one hundred sketches and four months of painting at the Gobelius tapestry works in Paris

At first sight this might appear surprising, and yet on closer examination it seems obvious that for Chagall, with his angels, his acrobats, his animals and his child-like world, the legend of the two abandoned children who a shepherd found being suckled by a sheep and a cow, and who grew up into the essence of pure youth to whom nature revealed love without recourse to human counsel, constituted a story that was bound to appeal. The notes of this pastoral melody may strike us as a trifle harsh after the psalms of the synagogue in Vitebsk, but they harmonize with the music of Chagall's genius. Work on the theme of *Daphnis and Chloe* occupied Chagall for a long time, and he later returned to it when he designed the scenery and costumes for Ravel's ballet based on this theme which was produced at the Paris Opéra.

166, 167 (*left*) Details of two of the canvas panels for the ceiling of the Paris Opéra

169 (*above*) *The Tree of Jesse*, 1960. A number of familiar Chagall motifs surround the façade of Notre-Dame

170 (*right*) *The Three Acrobats*, 1959

171 *The Tribe of Benjamin*. One of Chagall's twelve windows for the synagogue, Hadassah
Clinic, Jerusalem. Each of these round-arched windows is more than ten feet high

CHAPTER EIGHT

Chagall as a Religious Painter

Chassidism, the background in which Chagall was reared, is a form of Pietism. It is a religious way of life which begins with the observance of rituals covering the minutest details of daily life, but aims at achieving saintliness, especially in the figure of the religious leader, as set out in the Commentary on the Law. For Chassidism is an extension of the Cabbala, and the elders of the ghetto are the heirs of the rabbis who conceived this system, one of the richest and most powerful ever to have been conceived by the metaphysical imagination of man. It transports us to a world of emanation where all that exists here below resembles what is above, showing us the various degrees in which the light and warmth of the divine Presence can be experienced. This is certainly not pantheism – and the scholars hotly defend themselves against this interpretation – it is more a dynamism, a ceaseless application of divine thought to universal matters and to love.

The function of these righteous men of town and village, these venerable *zaddikim* that have so often appeared in Chagall's painting, is to preserve the tradition of meditation on the most profound mysteries, on names and letters, and on the most minute symbols in which the ineffable One makes Himself manifest. Even in extreme old age they still continue in their benevolent capacity, assisting in the endless sanctification of the days and the seasons of the year as well as all the occurrences and actions within the family, among friends and neighbours, in the house, the yard, the garden and the street, and extending to include even the tools of labour, furniture, and cattle and poultry. For sanctification and the obligation to sanctify are paramount, everything constitutes a feast-day, and each feast-

239

day must be celebrated, as must events such as betrothal, marriage, birth and burial. It is essential to liberate the redeeming feature hidden in all things, no matter how bad, the spark that lies buried in every man, no matter how ungodly or how evil. And this liberation is a labour of love.

Everything is a matter of love. All work is done in love. And without troubling to imitate the righteous men and the scholars in their efforts to verify this superb, absolute and single truth, it is enough to feel oneself a part of it. It is enough to feel that this is a great achievement. Moreover, this sentiment is one that must be felt with a burning heart, and the man within whom this heart beats must at every moment, with each breath that he takes and with every image that flits through his mind, feel convinced that he is moving towards the accomplishment of this same mission. He must feel that he is feeding the fire with which all other beings are aflame – whether they are beings within the planets, or animals or things – and he must gather up all these flames into one great conflagration.

Chagall is certainly not concerned with religious learning or with the minutiae of doctrine. However, though he is no saint or scholar, and though he is without theological or metaphysical training, as an essentially religious being he contributes in his own personal way to the sanctification of the world. He consequently possesses the power of an ordained priest, of a Levite fired with the flame of love for his tribe. It is this that is represented by the chromatic symbolism of the windows he made for the synagogue in Jerusalem (*Ill. 171*), with its bright yellow, the colour of the golden sun, the colour of jubilation. According to one famous Chassid, Rabbi Senior Zalman, the task of the Levites is 'to raise a song of joy and praise, with hymns and psalms, and with music and art'.

Chagall the musician and artist remained a stranger to learning; his activities were confined to painting. He held himself aloof from distinctions of doctrine and belief, from those that characterize the religion of his ancestors as well as from those that characterize other religions, and from the principal distinction between the revealed

172 *Cain and Abel*, 1911

Law of Judaism and the Christian New Testament. But in every religion, as in every idea, every dream, every thing, there is an inner fire that needs to be released, and in this way all religions are participants in total love. It is in this spirit that Chagall must unhesitatingly be described as a Jew and as a fundamentally religious being, as a religious man and a religious painter. The latter description applies, however, without reference to any one particular religion.

Chagall is unrivalled for the sensitive and moving way in which he has portrayed the spirit and not the doctrines of Judaism. He has conveyed the innermost and fundamental aspects of this spirit of Judaism, those aspects contributed by the Cabbalists and the Chassidim through their fervent study and the sublime sanctity of their lives. Moreover, there are few artists who, like Chagall, have painted religious feeling, religious reality in its very essence, without reference to any specific doctrine or denomination, in a portrayal of religion that goes beyond the established religions. This explains why one of the first figures Chagall thought of painting was that of Christ. It seems hardly necessary to point out that this was no instance of syncretism. Preoccupation with doctrinal conflicts and conciliations is not within the nature of this great soul.

During his youth in Russia, doubtless influenced by the icons, Chagall made a pen drawing of a *Crucifixion*. Later in 1912 while he was in Paris he developed this into a painting which was exhibited by Walden in 1913 under the title of *Dedicated to Christ*, and is known today as *Calvary* (*Ill. 30*). It is a huge picture without grace or proportion. An array of harsh and dull greens forms the background to this disconcerting image, with a giant-sized St John, a much smaller Virgin and a Christ represented in the form of a child. Apart from these canonical figures, the artist's imagination has introduced a bearded person, with a sombre and important air, who is carrying a long ladder, and in the background a ferryman in his boat, doubtless the ferryman of death, crossing over from the land of the living. This painting belongs to the group of Cubist works Chagall executed during this period, adding a somewhat strained note to their already highly dramatic character. Chagall subsequently did another smaller, much simpler and more animated version of this picture in a gouache, likewise entitled *Calvary*.

Once the theme of Christ on the cross has entered Chagall's work it is hardly surprising to find it reappearing during the troubled period preceding the war, and returning again in his American period. Firstly there is the great *White Crucifixion* (*Ill. 112*) of 1938. This time it is no longer a child being crucified, but the traditional bearded figure of Christ, who, swept forward by the catastrophe, appears in a great oblique shaft of light. This is the catastrophe of Jewry, foreshadowing the universal catastrophe. The victims fleeing hither and thither in this enormous, tumultuous picture are Jews, and at the foot of the Cross are the flames of the seven-branched

173 *Solitude*, 1933. In this painting from Chagall's Bible cycle we can recognize in the background the steeples of the Ilytch church and the houses of Vitebsk

candlestick. In a gouache done shortly after this, Chagall portrays himself in the act of painting a Crucifixion, with a wretched Jew moving across into the lower corner. In another gouache, the artist himself is crucified, one arm stretched out on the Cross, the other holding his palette. Finally, in *The Martyr* of the same year (1940) Christ no longer appears as a Jewish Christ, but simply as the Jew of contemporary reality, pilloried and tied to the stake. Here he appears surrounded by all of Chagall's traditional motifs, but in this instance they are convulsed by the agonies of the most terrible of Passions.

There is also the frightful and harrowing *Mexican Crucifixion*, and in 1943 the *Yellow Crucifixion*. Amidst the lurid blaze of *Obsession* (1943, *Ill. 130*) Christ appears upside-down as a green, barbaric-looking and disproportionately large figure. With the *Yellow Crucifixion* Chagall returns to a more traditional representation of Christ, with an opened Torah scroll at his side. *The Crucified* (1944, *Ill. 174*) are all Jews, a procession of stakes lining a village street in winter, presenting a black and unbearably desolate vision.

Two instances enable us to examine Chagall's curious mental process of substitution in action. The first is the *Flayed Ox* (1947, *Ill. 175*). The animal hangs with its two hind feet attached to the cross-bar of a gallows, its hide flaps loose and lifeless, but the head is alive and raises itself to drink from a tub of water below. This is set against the background of a snow-covered town. Vermilion and carmine flow into a stifling night of intensely mournful colouring – black, violet and dark blue, a blue that extends as far as the white of the snow. The few touches of green and yellow do not relieve the general sombreness of the whole. Clearly, this ox is related to the beasts the painter once saw in the butcher's shop of his childhood days. Here, however, it is a symbol of the martyr, the very personification of the sacrificed victim, a substitute for Christ on the Cross.

The other example is *Revolution* (*Ill. 106*). We have already seen how in 1943 Chagall decided to split up this huge composition into three separate pictures. The left-hand portion, completed in 1948, was to become *Resistance*, while the picture taken from the right-hand side became *Liberation*, and was not completed until 1952. Since we are examining Chagall's various representations of the Crucifixion, it is worth pointing out that this theme reappears in *Resistance*, thus linking the picture with the events which had shaken the world and had deeply moved the painter. We now come to the transformation of the central portion of the original painting, which became *Resurrection*, and was likewise completed in 1948. This section originally portrayed an uprising of the people, and this reappears in the new version, together with the man clasping the Torah, and the donkey seated on its chair. But the figure of Lenin in a curious posture with his head upside-down and feet in the air, symbolizing the Revolution, has been replaced by a tall and slender Christ on the Cross. Thus, Chagall equated the upheavals of the Revolution and the extremes to which it was resolutely and joyously prepared to go, on the

174 *The Crucified*, 1944

175 *Flayed Ox*, 1947. In this variation on the Crucifixion theme, the flying man with the knife recalls the green angel in one of Chagall's *Crucifixions*

one hand, with, on the other, the suffering and the tragedy of man.

'Revolution' was the original title of this picture, and the representation of the central figure conveyed everything arbitrary and unrestrained implicit in this title. For such an act, the act of revolution, could only be arbitrary and unrestrained. It was sudden, spontaneous and surprising, turning everything topsy-turvy. If we return to the causes of it we find iniquity, the conviction of the innocent, the torment of the poor, the pain and sacrifice of Christ the Man. This pain and sacrifice, moreover, will endure for ever. We have witnessed this in our own time, and have endured it. The image of it will remain forever – vast, irrefutable, a great vertical line in the centre of a page. Nevertheless it is called *Resurrection*. This is the message for a world whose lot is eternal suffering: there is still hope, hope that is likewise eternal. One does not exist without the other. Chagall's obsession with Christ is such that not only is this figure immediately recognizable in other figures painted by Chagall, but during this same period from 1948 to 1951 he also produced other *Crucifixions*, a *Holy Family* and a *Descent from the Cross* (*Ill. 176*).

Writers on Chagall – among them Franz Meyer in his comprehensive book on the artist – are agreed on the difficulty of interpreting paintings such as these. Let us return for a moment to our first, general impression. Here we have representations of the Jewish people. They are an expression of religious sentiment that goes beyond the differences between Judaism and Christianity, beyond the personalities and the doctrines of the two religions, and expresses rather what unites the two. Chagall takes no account of the differences and distinctions between them, but reduces all to the common denominator of human suffering.

The concept of suffering with which he identifies himself leads him to the common ground between religions. Yet he can feel no pity, for this would deny his personal involvement in the suffering. He never passes judgment, he does not reason and he is not concerned with knowing the facts. He observes, and in seeing things he becomes part of them, part of their wretchedness, their infinite suffering and their infinite patience. Thus he would not know what it is to feel pity. His way is to feel compassion or its twin emotion, sympathy. As a Jew he suffers with the Jews as well as with the 'King of the Jews' – words which appear in Hebrew characters beneath the traditional INRI on the inscription of one of the crucifixions – this 'King of the Jews' who to Christians is the son of God incarnate and who died on the Cross for the salvation of all men after he had taught them to love one another.

It is in the light of this universal commitment, in the light not of knowledge but of innocence, in the light of this reverence for love, that we must now consider the other specifically religious works of Chagall, beginning first of all with his Bible illustrations. They were, as I noted earlier, commissioned by Vollard after the completion of the *Fables* in 1931. That same year Chagall, accompanied by his wife and daughter, set sail on the S.S. Champollion for Palestine. In Haifa he met Hermann Struck, his former etching teacher, who had settled there. In Tel Aviv he was received by Dizengoff, the city's founder and mayor, one of the earliest and most celebrated pioneers. There Chagall came face to face with this extraordinary phenomenon of our time, the rebirth of Israel as a land to which the captive, the exiled and the wanderer were returning to build a homeland. Here the present existed side by side with the future. What Chagall also discovered, or rather re-discovered, were the ancient traditions familiar to him from his childhood days in Vitebsk. Here were the same faces and the same festivals, and his own memories intermingled with the oldest and most sacred memories of mankind. What had not been present in Vitebsk however – and what now transfigured his memories, giving them substance, colour and immediacy – was the light, the light that gives its name to the greatest book of Jewish mysticism, that illuminated the magnificent landscapes of the promised land, the eternally Holy Land, once lost and now regained. For this same land and light we see today witnessed events that go back to the creation of man as related in the Bible.

176 (*right*) *Descent from the Cross*, 1941. This gouache, painted in Connecticut, introduces a new motif into Chagall's portrayals of the Crucifixion

177 *Synagogue at Safad*, 1931. This and the work opposite were painted during Chagall's visit to Palestine in 1931–2

Chagall visited all the country's sites – Rachel's tomb, the Wailing Wall (*Ill. 178*), the synagogues and Safed, town of the Cabbalists. Oils and gouaches record these impressions, which are among the most moving in the whole of his life. Then he began work on the etchings. Between 1931 and the death of Vollard in 1939, he completed sixty-six plates. Thus for eight years Chagall was occupied with this enormous project. He returned to it after the war and in 1956 regarded the work as complete. Tériade published it in the following year. It is one of the finest masterpieces of the art of etching.

It is also one of the greatest expressions of the human soul. The size of the pictures corresponds to the overpowering majesty of the

178 *The Wailing Wall*, 1932

scenes depicted and to the importance of the characters. The naïve simplicity of Chagall's individual style emphasizes this quality of supreme grandeur and inevitably recalls that other sublime master in the portrayal of religious feeling, Rembrandt. To take one of the most overwhelming plates, *Abraham Weeping for Sarah*: is there not something in the undefinably humble, familiar and, as it were, un-gainly clumsiness that irresistibly recalls the gestures and postures of Rembrandt's figures? Is this not the same sort of dramatic ex-pression? This similarity between two such great souls surely leads us to an important truth, namely, that the sacred is nothing more than the human at its greatest.

Hegel has shown that what he calls romantic art, which is the art of the Christian era, necessarily brings anthropomorphism in its wake. Its content, he says, 'deals primarily with the fusion of the absolute and the divine with human subjectivity that is actually perceptible, and tangible'. This has meant that for centuries religious painting has concentrated on representing the life of Christ, for a religion founded upon incarnation lends itself most appropriately to pictorial representation. Although Chagall's roots lie in the Old Testament, he did not overlook this subject, since he introduced representations of the crucifixion into his painting. But obviously when he turned to the history of the Patriarchs, the Kings and the Prophets, these men directly connected with divine power, he was then fully able to achieve this fusion of human subjectivity with the divine, thereby creating works of religious art that are a contemporary contribution to the artistic epic of the spirit. The divine power with whom the Patriarchs, the Kings and the Prophets were in communion cannot be portrayed, but it can be felt in the gestures and postures, in the outward appearance and actions of these figures who have been singled out as holy men. This explains why they appear huge and disturbing to us. Yet they share our nature and are profoundly human. While they are not God incarnate, like the central figure of the New Testament, they are the incarnation of the feeling that man has for God and his awareness of being able to deal with God and conduct a dialogue with Him. It is this ultimate human power, this great human quality in man, that moves us in Chagall's *Bible*.

In 1950, while he was in Vence, the biblical figures once again began to stir the imagination of Chagall. But this time he considered them independently of the holy text which he had followed very closely while working on the etchings. The etchings had been planned as illustrations for the Book of Books. Now, however, the biblical figures were to speak for themselves, and the force of their message was to be delivered by their colour and enormous size. Abraham,

179 (*left*) *Elijah's Vision*. Etching and dry point. Plate 88 of *Bible*, 1931–6

Moses and David were clamouring to make a new appearance, and Chagall's imagination was obsessed by the insistence of their demand. What he had already expressed in the form of illustrations now had to be restated on a far grander and more monumental scale. Thus the artist developed his idea of the 'Bible message'. This consisted of huge canvases to be assembled in some place specially built for the purpose. These paintings were not intended as a decoration or ornament for an already existing building, such as a palace, museum, public hall, theatre, church or synagogue. They called for the erection of a place specifically built to house them. Not a place, like those listed above, devoted to any one specialized use, not a place of prayer, but a place beyond the limitations of any denominational restrictions or selective activities. It was to be a place of human assembly in which human beings gather and through which they pass, a place to visit for contemplation, for meditation, for communion – a place in which the experience of art may blend with the experience of what in its very broadest sense we choose to call religion.

In their movement, their vigour and their pathos, in the grandeur and the balance of their forms, and in the modulation of their colouring, the pictures of this *Bible Message* belong among the greatest products of the Baroque genius, prompting us to recall the great name of Tintoretto.

From his enthusiasm for ceramics Chagall turned to another art, stained-glass windows. Now he was Jacob grappling with the angel, though here the angel was light itself and Chagall enthusiastically came to grips with it. His first undertaking was to contribute two windows for the church at Assy. Then came an equally challenging commission from the Administration of Historic Monuments, inviting him (as they had previously invited Bissière and Jacques Villon) to design two large windows for the Gothic cathedral of Metz. (*Ills 181, 182* show two of the lancets.) He set to work with Charles and Brigitte Marq, from the famous old Simon workshop in Rheims, who from now on were to be his excellent collaborators.

181 *The Sacrifice of Abraham*, 1963. In creating his
stained-glass windows for
the Cathedral of Metz,
Chagall had to overcome
the considerable difficulty
of having to fit the glass
into the framework of the
existing tracery

182 *The Dream of Jacob*,
1963. Another of Chagall's
windows for Metz Cathe-
dral

Much patient preparatory work, including frequent visits to study Chartres cathedral, preceded his contribution, which was completed with the two splendid lancets, *Jeremiah* and *Exodus*. His windows depicting the twelve tribes of Israel, on the other hand, were intended for a modern structure, so that he was able to work on these in complete freedom, except that – and this is implicit in true creative freedom – he naturally had to relate his work to the design of the building and the purpose for which it was being erected. The windows (*Ill. 171*) were in fact for the synagogue of the Medical Centre which had been built near Jerusalem by Hadassah, the American Zionist Organization.

This religious work of Chagall's is as complete and monumental as was his *Bible* and his *Bible Message*, and it is placed where it belongs, in the ancestral holy land. As such it constitutes a conclusion to the entire religious expression of the artist, a conclusion that is also a return. At the beginning of this treatise I took great care not to describe Chagall's origins, since it seemed to me more appropriate to wait until these origins revealed themselves. Art consists of things shown and made manifest, and all the rest is literature. Now as the career and the work of this artist draws to a close, his origins appear to be having their influence on his work. Now that he is a creator he can create his origins.

The subject of the windows supports this contention that he is, as it were, re-creating his origins. For their subject deals with his own origins, the enumeration of the twelve sons of Jacob, from whom our entire history stems. This is not merely the history of Chagall's own people. In its exemplary and symbolic character, in its spirituality, in the echoes it has evoked, it is a history that is of interest to the whole of humanity. It is the sacred history of humanity. Not merely the history of a people strengthened in its alliance with God, from whom all emanates, but the history of mankind, conscious of its relationship with the universe and of its march through time regardless of the horrors and the calamities that have arisen along the way.

183 (*right*) *Blue Crucifixion*, 1941

All this vitalizes the organic world that constitutes the art of Chagall. In recent years Chagall's love of working in cycles has become even more pronounced. Seizing upon an idea that appears fundamental and essential to him, he develops it into a series that might well be extended indefinitely into time and space, forming a kind of architecture, an image of a vast universe.

In this way we see the motifs of Chagall's personal inner life – his memories, his obsessions, his symbols, all his faithful and dearly-loved friends – being brought to bear on the esoteric world of Hebraic symbolism. All the symbols of his irrepressible fantasy world now obediently and unprotestingly take up their appointed places in the Jerusalem windows, in the celestial light of Jerusalem. The trees, the plants and the animals – especially the mysterious animals whose exact meaning in Chagall's private mythology escapes us, but whose meaning does not need to be examined since it is less important than the outpouring of heart and dreams which it represents – all here derive their significance from the Scriptures. This significance is manifest in the harmony of the composition, a harmony that is often rich, perfect and luminous. Although these have become sacred figures, they are still quickened by the breath of Chagall's tenderness, they still are and will always remain beings created by his genius. It is this that permits his genius to submit in this instance to the demands of one specific religion, the religion in which he has been reared, and yet remain the religious genius *par excellence* in the most general and universal sense.

There are numerous instances of this wonderful harmony between a particular faith and an art which, in the act of serving it, overtakes the faith and aspires to ever greater objectives. In this context H. M. Rotermund very aptly observed that in Chagall's biblical themes it is always man that plays the dominant role and never a theological concept such as the sin of Adam. In the synagogue windows Chagall had to submit to the Mosaic law forbidding the representation of the human face. Therefore we see only objects, the usual symbols and components of Chagall's repertoire, and especially

184 *Resurrection at the River*, 1947. The zones of colour with their multitudinous life
in this painting have certain affinities with the illustrations for the *Arabian Nights*

185 *Jacob Wrestling with the Angel*, 1955

his beloved animals. Only the eyes and hands of man appear. Hands raised in blessing, hands lifting a crown, or hands that hold the *Shofar*, the means of expressing praise and exaltation through music. In the words of Jean Leymarie, in his book about the windows, man is symbolized by his two divine faculties, sight and touch. He is bereft of his face and disembodied, but this abstraction, this reduction of his form, is still the persistent theme in an essentially humanist art. Moreover, it is possible to detect in this stylization of man, imposed by doctrinal and conventional necessity, a far greater significance, the fulfilment of a deeper purpose in Chagall's spirituality. Thus the more conscious Chagall becomes of his Jewishness and his universalism, the more human and humanist he is, and the more religious he is in the unqualified, general meaning of the word.

Whatever the Scriptural significance may be of the donkey, the fishes, running water or flaming spheres, or whatever different significance Chagall's subconscious may have attributed to them, in the end this amounts to the same thing. As a poet descended from the prophets, Chagall knows that his deeds are akin to those by which an inspired people – his people – gives spiritual significance to the whole of creation. Thus the character of Chagall's specifically religious biblical work is the same as that of his so-called secular work, which deals only with his mysterious personal symbols, his memories, his childhood and all the joys and tribulations of his private destiny. Both are equally, essentially religious. For everything in the world, everything that is part of universal life, part of the life of a people, part of the life of a man, has significance. Everything is an expression of something. Everything is religion.

For observations such as these to be made in concluding a study of a painter, he must be of a quite exceptional nature and must possess two interdependent and particularly precious gifts: a rich subconscious and a lively imagination. We should consider these well, for they are indeed rare. When the two coincide and are effectively put to work they produce a psychic arrangement that is extremely unusual. This singularity is what astounds us and envelops us when we stop to consider Chagall's pictures, their colours, their shapes, the compelling strangeness of all that they have to say.

Chagall resides on the inside of all this. Unlike certain quite different, but equally valid, artists, he does not detach himself from his work. Thus one cannot question him about it; his replies will always be couched in plastic terms. These replies are nevertheless of great interest since he is a prodigious artist, a modest and skilful craftsman, as well as a powerful and tireless creator, growing increasingly bold and fertile with advancing years (the most recent example of this being the splendid ceiling he has executed for the Paris Opéra, *Ills 166–8*) and with a deep understanding of the subtle secrets of painting. On all else, however, he keeps his silence, for the rest belongs to his inner world and must remain there.

Thus he defends this private world and does so by his personal charm and his character, which emerge most strikingly in his narrative and poetic fantasy. In his dealings with others Chagall may appear to resemble those equally charming creatures of aerial wonder from his own world of fable. This same delightful Chagall has spoken somewhere of 'this bleating love' that he bears 'for all people indiscriminately'. An endearing statement, despite its wickedness, defining this Chagallian tenderness and all that we infer from the lovable and ingenuous childhood portrayed in so many of this miraculous poet's pictures. But from this angelic state of early purity to the burning intensity of the flame of love, it is the same heart expressing its emotions, an essentially religious heart for which nothing exists that is not in some way linked and related to universal life.

A heart such as this is the personification of good will. If it were not so, it would not find love in the rustling of the tiniest blade of grass and in the noise of the smallest of nature's creatures, recognizing in them the driving impulse behind the greatest and most imperious forces. Strengthened by this awareness, good is able to resist the onslaughts of evil. The latter has displayed its destructive folly

186 *Offerings,* 1959

since the beginnings of the world, and the Old and the New Testaments have transmitted to successive generations the events and the characters in this perpetual and deadly war conducted by evil against the forces of love. Our century has in turn known and experienced its cruel impact.

It is this interdependence of the periods of history that is expressed in the work of Chagall. There are pictures corresponding to all the different ages, and one will reflect the essence of another. In so doing they are invested with the form of the creatures, the shapes, the colours, the symbols, the couples, the birds, the spheres – all the wondrous inhabitants of the poet's mental space, the space of his destiny, universal space. In this space, as in these different ages, everything is continual animation and thereby leads to a total unity of the soul.

Chronology

1887 July 7 born Vitebsk

1906 Studied art in Vitebsk with Pen

1907 Entered the School of the Imperial Society for the Protection of Arts, Saint Petersburg

1908 Studied at Saidenberg's private school, then at Bakst's

1909 Continued to study under Bakst, long visits to Vitebsk. Met Bella Rosenfeld, his future wife

1910–13 First Paris period. First studio in the Impasse du Maine; end of 1911, moved to 'La Ruche'

1912 First exhibited in the Salon des Indépendants and the Salon d'Automne

1914 One-man show in 'Der Sturm' Gallery, Berlin. Visit to Vitebsk

1915 Married Bella, moved to Saint Petersburg

1916 Ida born

1917 After October Revolution, returned to Vitebsk

1918 September, appointed Commissar for Art in the 'government' of Vitebsk

1919 January, Vitebsk Academy founded under Chagall's directorship

1920 May, resigned as Director following quarrel with Suprematists. Moved to Moscow. Stage designs, murals for Kameray State Jewish Theatre, sets and costumes for *The Miniatures* by Sholem Aleichem

1922 Left Russia for Berlin. Etchings for *My Life*

1923 Autumn, moved to Paris

1924 First retrospective exhibition held at Galerie Barbazanges-Hodebert. Summer visit to Brittany. Worked on Gogol's *Dead Souls*

1925 Summer at Montchauvet, near Mantes

1926 At Mourillon near Toulon and Lac Chambon in the Auvergne. Gouaches for the *Fables* of La Fontaine

1928 Etchings for the *Fables* (until 1931)

1930 At Peyra-Cava

1931 Journey to Palestine. Began Bible etchings (until 1938 and from 1952 to 1956)

1932 Journey to Holland

1933 Large retrospective exhibition at the Kunsthalle, Basle

1934 Visit to Spain

1935 Visit to Poland for the inauguration of the Jewish Institute at Vilna

1937 Stayed at Villeneuve-lès-Avignon. Visited Florence and Tuscany

1939 Carnagie Prize. At Saint-Dyé in the Loire district

1940 Moved to Gordes, Haute Provence

1941 Left for the United States, arriving in New York on June 23

1942 Visit to Mexico. Sets and costumes for *Aleko*

1944 September, Bella died

1945 At Sag Harbour. Sets and costumes for *The Firebird*

1946 At High Falls. Retrospective exhibition at the Museum of Modern Art, New York. First post-war visit to Paris

1947 Exhibition in the Musée National d'Art Moderne, Paris, the first of many exhibitions in European galleries in the succeeding years

1948 Returned to France for good in August. Moved from Paris to Orgeval near Saint-Germain-en-Laye. Lithographs for *Arabian Nights*

1949 To Saint-Jean-Cap-Ferrat

1950 Settled at 'Les Collines', Vence. Ceramics

1951 Journey to Israel. First sculptures

1952 Married to Vava Brodsky. First Visit to Greece. Visited Italy

1953 (until 1956) Paris series

1954 Second Journey to Greece. Began lithographs for *Daphnis and Chloe*

1958 Chicago. Lectured at the University. Sets and costumes for *Daphnis and Chloe*

1959 Honorary doctorate from the University of Glasgow

1960 Honorary doctorate from Brandeis University, at Copenhagen. First of the two windows for Metz Cathedral

1962 Journey to Israel for installation of the stained-glass window at the Medical Centre near Jerusalem. Honorary citizen of Vence

1963 Journey to Washington. Model for the ceiling of the Paris Opéra.

1964 Opéra ceiling unveiled

1965 Honorary doctorate from Notre Dame. Began costumes and sets for New York Metropolitan production of Mozart's *Magic Flute*. Worked on murals for Metropolitan Opera House façade

Short Bibliography

GUSTAVE COQUIOT, *Cubistes, Passéistes, Futuristes*, Ollendorff. Paris, 1941. New edition 1923

THEODOR DAUBLER, *Der neue Standpunkt*, Insel-Verlag, Leipzig, 1919

MAURICE RAYNAL, *Anthologie de la peinture en France de 1906 à nos jours*, Ed. Montaigne, Paris, 1927. Translated into English: *Modern French Painters*, Brentano's, New York, 1928

Sélection. Special Chagall issue, No. VI., Antwerp, 1929 (Texts by Chagall, G. Charensol, P. Courthion, J. Delteil, A. Efross, W. George, P. Fierens, J. Maritain, M. Raynal, A. de Ridder, A. Vollard, K. With)

RENÉ SCHWOB, *Chagall et l'âme juive*, Corrêa, Paris, 1930

A. M. HAMMACHER, *Marc Chagall*, Ed. 'De Spieghel', Amsterdam, and 'Het Kompas', Antwerp, 1935

ANDRÉ BRETON, '*Le surréalisme et la peinture*', translation published in: Peggy Guggenheim, *Art of this Century*, New York, 1942.

MICHEL GEORGES-MICHEL, *Peintres, sculpteurs que j'ai connus, 1900–1942*, Brentano's, New York, 1942

RAISSA MARITAIN, *Marc Chagall*, Ed. de la Maison Française, New York, 1943

SIDNEY JANIS, *Abstract and Surrealist Art in America*. Raynal and Hitchcock, New York, 1944

G. JEDLICKA, *Begegnungen mit Künstlern der Gegenwart*, Erlenbach, Zurich, 1945

LIONELLO VENTURI, *Marc Chagall*, Pierre Matisse, New York, 1945

BERNARD DORIVAL, *Les étapes de la peinture française contemporaine*, III, Gallimard, Paris, 1946

JAMES JOHNSON SWEENEY, *Marc Chagall*, Museum of Modern Art, New York, 1946

LÉON DEGAND and PAUL ELUARD, *Chagall, peintures 1942–1945*, Ed. du Chêne, Paris, 1947. English edition: Lindsay Drummond, London, 1947

MAURICE RAYNAL, *Peintres du XXᵉ siècle*, Skira, Geneva, 1947

RAISSA MARITAIN, *Chagall ou l'orage enchanté*, Ed. des Trois Collines, Geneva

UMBRO APOLLONIO, *Chagall*, Alfieri, Venice, 1949

MICHAEL AYRTON, *Chagall*, Faber and Faber, London, 1950

RAYMOND COGNIAT, *De David à Picasso*, Ed. La Diane Française, Nice, 1950

LIONELLO VENTURI, *Painting and Painters; how to look at pictures from Giotto to Chagall*, Scribner's, New York, 1945.

JACQUES LASSAIGNE, *Histoire de la peinture moderne: de Picasso au surréalisme*, Skira, Geneva, 1950

CHARLES ESTIENNE, *Chagall*, French and English edition, Somogy, Paris, 1951

J. KLOOMOK, *Marc Chagall, his life and work*, Philosophical Library, New York, 1951

GEORG SCHMIDT, *Chagall*, Fernand Hazan, Paris, 1952

GEORG SCHMIDT, *Chagall*, Holbein-Verlag, Basle, 1955

GEORG SCHMIDT, *Kleine Geschichte der modernen Malerei, von Daumier bis Chagall*, Fr. Reinhardt-Verlag, Basle, 1955 (French edition: Ed. du Griffon, Neuchâtel, 1956)

Dictionnaire de la peinture contemporaine (*Chagall* by Jacques Lassaigne), Hazan, Paris, 1955. Methuen, London, 1956

WERNER HAFTMANN, *Malerei im 20. Jahrhundert*, Prestel-Verlag, Munich, 1955. American edition: Frederick A. Praeger, 1960

BERNARD DORIVAL, *Les peintres du XXe siècle: du Cubisme à l'Abstraction*, Tisné, Paris, 1957

JACQUES LASSAIGNE, *Chagall*, Maeght, Paris, 1957

MARCEL JEAN, *Histoire de la peinture surréaliste*, Ed. du Seuil, Paris, 1959. American edition: Grove Press, New York, 1960

FRANÇOIS MATHEY, *Marc Chagall, 1909–1918, 1918–1939* (Petite encyclopédie de l'art, 2 vol., Hazan, Paris, 1959)

HERBERT READ, *A Concise History of Modern Painting*, Thames and Hudson, London, 1959; Frederick A. Praeger, New York

MARCEL BRION, *Chagall*, Somogy, Paris, 1959

JEAN CASSOU, *Panorama des arts plastiques contemporains*, Gallimard, Paris, 1960

JACQUES CHAPIRO, *La Ruche*, Flammarion, Paris, 1960

RENÉ HUYGHE, *Art and the Spirit of Man*, Thames and Hudson, London, 1960

EDOUARD RODITI, *Dialogues on Art*, Secker and Warburg, London, 1960

ROBERT ROSENBLUM, *Cubism and 20th Century Art*, Harry N. Abrams, New York, 1961

FRANZ MEYER, *Marc Chagall*, Thames and Hudson, London; Harry N. Abrams, New York, 1961

ELISA DEBENEDETTI, *Il mito di Chagall*, Longanesi, Milan, 1962

JEAN LEYMARIE, *Les Vitraux pour Jérusalem de Marc Chagall*, André Sauret, Monte Carlo, 1962. American edition: *The Jerusalem Windows* [by] *Marc Chagall*, George Braziller, New York, 1962

Articles, poems, interviews

MARC CHAGALL, *Reflections on art* (in Russian), *Witebskvi Listok*, No. 1091, January 8, 1919

MARC CHAGALL, *The revolution in art* (in Russian), *Revoluzionnoje Iskustwo*, Vitebsk, No. 1, p. 2–3, 1919

MARC CHAGALL, *Reflections on the People's Fine Arts Academy, Vitebsk* (on the occasion of the first exhibition by Chagall's pupils). In Russian. *Schkola revoluzia*, Vitebsk, Nos 24–25, August 16, 1919

GEORGES CHARENSOL, *Chez Marc Chagall* (Interview), *Paris-Journal*, May 16, 1924

FLORENT FELS, *Propos d'artistes*, Ed. La Renaissance du Livre, Paris, 1925

ANDRÉ SALMON, '*Marc Chagall*', *L'Art Vivant*, Paris, 1, No. 2, 1925

MARC CHAGALL, *My first teacher, Pen* (in Russian), *Razsviet*, Paris, January 30, 1927

JACQUES GUENNE, *Marc Chagall* (Interview), *L'Art Vivant*, Paris, 3, No. 72, December 15, 1927

MAURICE RAYNAL, *Anthologie de la peinture en France de 1906 à nos jours*, Ed. Montaigne, Paris, 1927. American edition: *Modern French Painters*, Brentano's, New York, 1928

MARC CHAGALL, *My work in the Jewish Theatre of Moscow* (in Yiddish), *Di Idisze Welt*, Vilna, 1928

MARC CHAGALL, '*Delacroix et nos peintres*', *L'Intransigeant*, Paris, June 9, 1930

LADISLAS SZECKI, '*Marc Chagall*', *Kunst und Künstler*, Berlin, September 1931

PIERRE COURTHION, *Marc Chagall* (Interview), *Les Nouvelles Littéraires*, Paris, April 30, 1932

MARC CHAGALL, *Réponse à une enquête: 'Pouvez-vous dire quelle est la rencontre capitale de votre vie?'*, *Minotaure*, Paris, Nos 3–4, 1933

MARC CHAGALL, *Réponse à une enquête:* '*Sur la crise de la peinture*', *Beaux-Arts*, Brussels, August 19, 1935

MARC CHAGALL, *Réponse à une enquête:* '*Sur l'art d'aujourd'hui*', *Cahiers d'Art*, Paris, Nos 1–4, 1935

RAYMOND ABEL, '*Interview with Marc Chagall*'. *The League*, New York, No. 1, April 1942

MARC CHAGALL, '*In honour of Jacques Maritain*', *Jewish Frontier*, New York, February 1943

MARC CHAGALL, '*Message aux peintres français*', *Le Spectateur des Arts*, Ed. René Drouin, Paris, December 1944

JAMES JOHNSON SWEENEY, '*An Interview with Marc Chagall*', *Partisan Review*, New York, 11, No. 1, Winter 1944

MARC CHAGALL, '*Quelques impressions sur la peinture française*', Lecture at Mount Holyoke College, August 1943, *Renaissance, revue trimestrielle de l'Ecole des Hautes Etudes de New York*, Vol. II–III, 1944–45

MARC CHAGALL, '*L'Art de la rectitude et de la clarté*', Talk given at reception given by ICOR in honour of Chagall and Itzik Feffer, April 30, 1944, *Naje Lehn*, New York, XVIII, No. 6, June 1945

BELLA CHAGALL, *Di ershte Bagegenish*, Book League of the Jewish People Fraternal Order, I.W.O., New York, 1947. Preface by Marc Chagall

MARC CHAGALL, *Lettre to S. Rosengart*, from Orgeval, June 16, 1949, Exhibition catalogue, Lucerne 1949

MARC CHAGALL, *Five Poems*, in '*Di Goldene Keyt*', Tel Aviv, 1951

GISÈLE D'ASSAILLY, *Visite à Chagall* (Interview), *Le Figaro Littéraire*, March 1, 1952, Paris

MARC CHAGALL, *Hommage à Matisse*, The Yale Library Magazine, New Haven, 1955

MARC CHAGALL, *Lecture at the University of Chicago*, Chicago, February 1958

List of Illustrations

Dimensions are given in inches, height preceding width. Location of artist's signature is indicated by abbreviations: l.l. (lower left), l.r. (lower right), l.c. (lower centre), u.r. (upper right)

1 *Woman with Basket*, 1906–7
Signed l.l.
Oil on cardboard, $26^3/_4 \times 20^1/_8$
Private collection, Moscow

2 *Peasant Woman*, 1907
Signed l.r.
Oil on canvas, $20^1/_4 \times 15^5/_8$
Artist's collection

3 *The House in the Park*, 1908
Signed l.r.
Oil on canvas, $24 \times 20^7/_8$
Private collection, France

4 *Self-portrait with Brushes*, 1909
Unsigned
Oil on canvas, $22^1/_2 \times 18^7/_8$
Collection Alport, Oxford, England

5 *Portrait of my Fiancée in Black Gloves*, 1909
Signed l.r.
Oil on canvas, $34^5/_8 \times 25^5/_8$
Kunstmuseum, Basle

6 *The Holy Family*, 1909
Signed l.r.
Oil on canvas, $39^1/_8 \times 35^3/_8$
Artist's collection

7 *The Dead Man*, 1908
Signed l.r.
Oil on canvas, $27^1/_8 \times 34^1/_4$
Private collection, France

8 *Birth*, 1910
Signed l.r.
Oil on canvas, $25^5/_8 \times 35^1/_4$
Artist's collection

9 *Dedicated to my Fiancée*, 1911
Signed l.l.
Oil on canvas, $77^1/_8 \times 45$
Kunstmuseum, Berne

10 *Russian Village, from the Moon*, 1911
Signed l.r.
Oil on canvas, $49^5/_8 \times 40^1/_8$
Private collection, Krefeld, Westphalia

11 *The Holy Carter*, 1911
Signed u.r.
Oil on canvas, $58^1/_4 \times 46^1/_4$
Private collection, Krefeld, Westphalia

12 *I and the Village*, 1911
Signed l.l.
Oil on canvas, $75^1/_4 \times 59^1/_4$
Museum of Modern Art, New York (Mrs Simon Guggenheim Fund)

13 *The Sleigh*, 1911
Signed l.r.
Gouache on paper, $6^3/_4 \times 7^1/_2$
Collection Dr Roger Vokaer, Brussels

273

14 *Full Moon*, 1911
Signed l.l.
Gouache on paper, $7^{1}/_{4} \times 5^{7}/_{8}$
Collection Klipstein and Kornfeld, Berne

15 *To Russia, Asses and Others*, 1911
Signed l.c.
Oil on canvas, $61^{3}/_{8} \times 48$
Musée National d'Art Moderne, Paris

16 *The Birth*, 1911
Signed l.r.
Oil on canvas, $18^{1}/_{8} \times 14^{1}/_{8}$
Private collection, Basle

17 *Madonna with Child*, 1911
Signed l.r.
Gouache on cardboard, $9^{3}/_{4} \times 5^{3}/_{4}$
Collection E. W. Kornfeld, Berne

18 *The Soldier*, 1911
Signed l.l.
Gouache on paper, $11^{1}/_{2} \times 8$
Collection Mr and Mrs Victor Babin, Cleveland, Ohio

19 *Man with Scythe*, 1911
Gouache on paper
Collection Mr and Mrs Fredric R. Mann, Philadelphia

20 *The Mirror*, 1911-2
Signed l.r.
India ink and watercolour on paper, $10^{1}/_{2} \times 8$
Los Angeles County Museum, Collection Mr and Mrs William Preston Harrison

21 *The Wedding*, 1911
Signed l.l.
Ink and pastel on paper, $10^{1}/_{4} \times 13^{1}/_{4}$
Collection Mr and Mrs Victor Babin, Cleveland, Ohio

22 *Still Life with Lamp*, 1910
Signed l.r.
Oil on canvas, $31^{7}/_{8} \times 17^{3}/_{4}$
Galerie Rosengart, Lucerne

23 *Nude with Raised Arm*, 1911
Signed l.r.
Gouache on brown paper, 9×12
Beyeler Gallery, Basle

24 *Composition*, 1912
Signed l.l.
Gouache on paper
Collection M. Planque, Paris

25 *The Cattle Dealer*, 1912
Signed l.r.
Oil on canvas, $37^{3}/_{4} \times 78^{3}/_{4}$
Kunstmuseum, Basle

26 *The Fiddler*, 1912-3
Signed l.c.
Oil on canvas, $72^{1}/_{2} \times 58^{1}/_{2}$
Stedelijk Museum, Amsterdam

27 *Peasant Eating*
Signed l.r.
Pen drawing on paper, $11^{1}/_{4} \times 8^{7}/_{8}$
Private collection, The Netherlands

28 *My Parents*, 1912
Signed l.r.
Gouache on paper, $20^{1}/_{2} \times 13^{3}/_{8}$
Collection Georges Daelemans, Brussels

29 *Still Life*, 1912
Signed on back
Oil on canvas, $24^3/_4 \times 30^3/_4$
Collection Eric Estorick, London

30 *Calvary*, 1912
Signed l.r.
Oil on canvas, $68^1/_2 \times 75^1/_4$
Museum of Modern Art, New
York (Lillie P. Bliss Bequest)

31 *Orpheus*, 1912
Signed l.l.
Oil on canvas, $19^3/_8 \times 22^1/_4$
Solomon R. Guggenheim Mu-
seum, New York

32 *The Lovers*, 1913–4
Signed l.r.
Oil on canvas, $41^3/_8 \times 51^1/_8$
Collection A. A. Juviler, New
York

33 *Woman*
India ink drawing, brush and pen
on paper

34 *Self-portrait in Front of House*, 1914
Signed l.r.
Oil on canvas, $19^1/_2 \times 14^7/_8$
Private collection, Paris

35 *Over Vitebsk*, 1914
Signed l.r.
Oil on cardboard, mounted on
canvas, $28^3/_4 \times 36^1/_2$
Collection Ayala and Sam Zacks,
Toronto

36 *Paris through the Window*, 1913
Signed l.l.
Oil on canvas, $48^1/_4 \times 54^3/_4$
Solomon R. Guggenheim Mu-
seum, New York

37 *Pregnant Woman*, 1912–3
Signed l.c.
Oil on canvas, $76^3/_8 \times 45^1/_4$
Stedelijk Museum, Amsterdam

38 *Self-portrait at the Easel*, 1914
Signed l.r.
Oil on canvas, $28^3/_8 \times 18^1/_2$
Collection Ilya Ehrenburg

39 *Burning House*, 1913
Signed l.r.
Oil on canvas, $42^1/_8 \times 47^1/_2$
Solomon R. Guggenheim Mu-
seum, New York

40 *Jew in Green*, 1914
Signed l.l.
Oil on cardboard, $39^3/_8 \times 31^1/_2$
Collection Charles Im Obersteg,
Geneva

41 *The Praying Jew*, 1914
Signed l.r.
Oil on cardboard, mounted on
canvas, $39^3/_8 \times 31^7/_8$
Collection Charles Im Obersteg,
Geneva

42 *Lilies of the Valley*, 1916
Signed l.l.
Oil on cardboard
Private collection, Moscow

43 *Wedding*, 1917
Signed l.r.
Oil on cardboard, $39^3/_8 \times 46^7/_8$
Tretyakov Gallery, Moscow

44 *Vitebsk Seen from Mount Zadunov*,
1917
Signed l.r.
Oil on canvas, $24^3/_8 \times 32^1/_4$
Collection Mr and Mrs Perry R.
Pease, New York

45 *The Blue House*, 1917
Signed l.r.
Oil on canvas, 24 × 38 1/8
Musée des Beaux-Arts, Liège

46 *The Poet Reclining*, 1915
Signed l.l.
Oil on cardboard, 18 1/4 × 18 1/2
Tate Gallery, London

47 *Lovers in Blue*, 1914
Signed (in Russian) l.l.c.
Oil on cardboard, 19 × 17 1/2
Private collection, Leningrad

48 *Over the Town*, 1917–8
Signed l.r.
Oil on canvas, 61 3/8 × 83 1/2
Tretyakov Gallery, Moscow

49 *The Birthday*, 1915
Signed (in Russian) l.r.
Oil on cardboard, 31 3/4 × 39 1/8
Museum of Modern Art, New
York (Lillie P. Bliss Bequest)

50 *Promenade*, 1913
Signed l.r.
Oil on canvas, 66 7/8 × 64 1/2
State Russian Museum, Leningrad

51 *Double Portrait with Wineglass*,
1917
Signed l.r.
Oil on canvas, 91 3/4 × 53 1/2
Musée National d'Art Moderne,
Paris

52 *Street at Night*
India ink on paper
Private collection, Klagenfurt,
Austria

53 *Wounded Soldier*, 1914
Signed (in Russian) u.r.
Oil on cardboard, 14 1/8 × 19 1/4
Collection Mary K. Woodworth,
Bryn Mawr College, Bryn Mawr,
Pennsylvania

54 *Young Soldiers*, 1914
Signed (in Russian) l.r.
Oil on paper, 20 1/8 × 15
Private collection, Malmö

55 *Wounded Soldier*, 1914
Signed l.r.
Pencil and pen on paper, 8 5/8 × 7 1/8
Private collection, Moscow

56 *The Traveller*, 1917
Signed l.r.
Oil on cardboard, 12 1/4 × 18 1/8
Private collection, Moscow

57 *Acrobat*, 1914
Signed l.l.
Oil on cardboard, 16 1/2 × 12 7/8
Albright-Knox Art Gallery,
Buffalo

58 *Man Carrying Street*
Signed l.l.
India ink drawing on paper,
12 5/8 × 8 5/8
Private collection

59 Costume design for a play by
Sholem Aleichem
Signed l.r.
Watercolour on paper, 11 × 7 1/2
Artist's collection

60 Illustration for Gogol's *Dead Souls*
Signed l.r.
Gouache and watercolour
O'Hana Gallery, London

61 Scene design for Gogol's *The Inspector General*
Signed l.l.
Pen, pencil and watercolour on paper, $11\,^1/_4 \times 13\,^1/_2$
Artist's collection

62 *The Actor*
Signed l.l. 'Marc' and l.r. 'Chagall'
Pen drawing, India ink on paper
Private collection, Chicago

63 *The Yellow Room*, 1911
Signed l.r.
Oil on canvas, $21\,^1/_8 \times 44\,^1/_8$
Collection R.F.T. Dr Paul Hänggi, Basle

64 *The Drunkard*, 1911–2
Signed l.r.
Oil on canvas, $33\,^1/_2 \times 45\,^1/_4$
Collection Hans Neumann, Caracas

65 *Little Parlour*, 1908
Signed l.r.
Oil on paper, mounted on canvas, $8\,^7/_8 \times 11\,^3/_8$
Private collection, France

66 *The Harvest*, 1910
Signed l.r.
Oil on canvas, $23\,^5/_8 \times 31\,^7/_8$
Perls Gallery, New York

67 *Studio*, 1910
Signed l.c.
Oil on canvas, $23\,^5/_8 \times 28\,^3/_4$
Artist's collection

68 *Self-portrait with Seven Fingers*, 1912
Signed l.l.
Oil on canvas, $50\,^3/_8 \times 42\,^1/_8$
Stedelijk Museum, Amsterdam

69 *Reclining Nude*, 1911
Signed l.l.
Gouache on cardboard, $9\,^1/_2 \times 13\,^5/_8$
Collection Eric Estorick, London

70 *Homage to Apollinaire*, 1911–2
Signed u.c.
Oil on canvas, $42\,^7/_8 \times 78$
Stedelijk van Abbe Museum, Eindhoven, The Netherlands

71 *The Soldier Drinks*, 1912
Signed l.r.
Oil on canvas, $43\,^1/_4 \times 37\,^3/_8$
Solomon R. Guggenheim Museum, New York

72 *The Poet*, 1911
Signed l.l.
Oil on canvas, $77\,^5/_8 \times 57\,^1/_2$
Philadelphia Museum of Art (Louise and Walter Arensberg Collection)

73 *Adam and Eve*, 1912
Signed l.l.
Oil on canvas, $63\,^1/_4 \times 42\,^7/_8$
City Art Museum of St Louis

74 *Apollinaire*, 1911
Signed l.r.
Pencil on paper, $13 \times 10\,^1/_4$
Artist's collection

75 *Adam and Eve*, 1911–2
Study for *Homage to Apollinaire*
Signed l.l. 'Marc' and l.r. 'Chagall'
Gouache on paper, $10\,^7/_8 \times 9\,^1/_2$
Private collection, Basle

76 *Sketch for Homage to Apollinaire*, 1910
Pencil on paper, $5\,^1/_8 \times 4\,^3/_4$
Artist's collection

77 *Profile at the Window*, 1919
Signed l.l.
Oil on cardboard, $6^1/_2 \times 8^5/_8$
Artist's collection

78 *A Gentleman*, 1920
Signed l.l.
Pen drawing, India ink,
$18^1/_2 \times 12^5/_8$
Private collection, France

79 *Chichikov's Arrival*, illustration for
Gogol's *Dead Souls*
Etching and dry point, $8^7/_8 \times 11^1/_8$
Paris: Tériade, 1948

80 Scene design for Synge's *The Playboy of the Western World*, 1920
Signed l.r.
Pencil and gouache on paper,
$13^3/_4 \times 20^1/_8$
Artist's collection

81 *Ida at the Window*, 1924
Signed l.r.
Oil on canvas, $41^3/_8 \times 29^1/_2$
Stedelijk Museum, Amsterdam

82 *Lovers under Lilies*, 1922–5
Signed l.l.
Oil on canvas, $45^3/_4 \times 35^1/_8$
Perls Gallery, New York

83 *Lovers with Flowers*, 1926
Signed l.r.
Oil on canvas, $36^1/_4 \times 28^3/_4$
Collection Arturo Deana, Venice

84 *The Open Window*, 1926
Signed l.r.
Pencil and gouache on paper,
$25^5/_8 \times 19^5/_8$
Collection Prof. Dr H. Kräyenbühl, Zurich

85 *Bride and Groom with Eiffel Tower*,
1928
Signed l.l.
Oil on canvas, $35 \times 45^5/_8$
Collection M. Roncey, Paris

86 *Bella with a Carnation*, 1925
Signed l.r.
Oil on canvas, $39^3/_8 \times 31^1/_2$
Collection Ida Meyer-Chagall,
Basle

87 *Double Portrait*, 1924–5
Signed l.r.
Oil on canvas, $51^1/_8 \times 37$
Collection Katia Granoff, Paris

88 *Bella in Green*, 1934–5
Signed l.r.
Oil on canvas, $39^3/_8 \times 31^7/_8$
Stedelijk Museum, Amsterdam

89 *Around Her*, 1945
Signed l.r.
Oil on canvas, $51^5/_8 \times 42^7/_8$
Musée National d'Art Moderne,
Paris

90 *Donkey Covered with Lion's Skin*,
1926
Signed l.r.
Illustration for La Fontaine's
Fables
Gouache on paper, 19×16
O'Hana Gallery, London

91 *The Clown with the Donkey*, 1927
Signed l.r.
Gouache on paper, $25^5/_8 \times 19^5/_8$
Collection G. Pinkus, Beverly
Hills, California

92 *To Charlie Chaplin*, 1929
Signed l.l.
Pen drawing, India ink on paper,
16⁷/₈ × 11
Private collection

93 *On the Sofa*, 1929
Signed l.r.
Oil on canvas, 31⁷/₈ × 25⁵/₈
Collection M. Haakon Onstad,
Munkedal, Sweden

94 *The Dream*, 1927
Signed l.r.
Oil on canvas, 31⁷/₈ × 39³/₈
Musée d'Art Moderne, Paris

95 *The Satyr and the Wanderer*, 1927
Illustration for La Fontaine's *Fables*
Gouache on paper, 16 × 19³/₄
Los Angeles County Museum
(Gift of Mrs H. English)

96 *Fruits and Flowers*, 1929
Signed l.l.
Oil on canvas, 39³/₈ × 31⁷/₈
Private collection, Paris

97 *Nude over Vitebsk*, 1933
Signed l.l.
Oil on canvas, 34¹/₄ × 44¹/₈
Private collection, Paris

98 *Lovers in Moonlight*, 1926–8
Signed l.r.
Gouache on paper, 25⁷/₈ × 19¹/₃
Collection Herman E. Cooper,
New York

99 *The Fiancée*, 1926
Signed l.r.
Gouache on paper
Collection Georges Charenzel,
Paris

100 *The Bridal Couple*, 1930
Signed l.r.
Oil on canvas, 58¹/₄ × 31⁷/₈
Collection Mr and Mrs Le Ray
Berdeau, Palm Beach

101 *Flowers*, 1930
Signed l.l.
Oil on canvas
Collection Mr and Mrs Isadore
Levin, Palm Beach

102 *Church at Chambon*, 1926
Signed l.r.
Gouache on paper, 25⁵/₈ × 20¹/₈
Boymans van Beuningen Museum, Rotterdam

103 *Return from the Synagogue*,
1925–7
Signed l.l.
Oil on cardboard, mounted on
canvas, 28³/₈ × 36¹/₄
Collection Maurice Lefèbvre-
Foinet, Paris

104 *The Cellist*, 1939
Signed l.l.
Oil on canvas, 39³/₈ × 28³/₄
Private collection, London

105 *Snow-covered Church*, 1928–9
Signed l.r.
Gouache on paper, 23⁵/₈ × 20¹/₈
Detroit Institute of Arts

106 Study for *The Revolution*, 1937
Signed l.r.
Oil on canvas
Private collection

107 *Liberation*, 1952
Signed l.c.
Oil on canvas, 66¹/₈ × 34⁵/₈
Private collection, France

108 *The Yoke*, 1930
Signed l.l.
Gouache on paper, 26³/₈×20¹/₂
Collection Mr and Mrs Victor
Babin, Cleveland, Ohio

109 *White Lilacs*, 1930
Signed l.l.
Oil on canvas, 36¹/₄×29
Collection Nathan Cummings,
Chicago

110 *Mother*, 1935
Signed l.l.
Gouache and pastel on paper,
17¹/₄×11¹/₈
O'Hana Gallery, London

111 *The Red Cock*, 1940
Signed l.r.
Oil on canvas, 28³/₈×35⁷/₈
Collection Mary E. Johnson,
Glendale, Ohio

112 *White Crucifixion*, 1938
Signed l.r.
Oil on canvas, 61×55
Art Institute of Chicago, Gift
of Alfred S. Alschuler

113 *Blue Air*, 1938
Signed l.l.
Oil on canvas, 45×34
Collection Dr Ruth Stephan,
Greenwich, Connecticut

114 *The Three Candles*, 1938–40
Signed l.r.
Oil on canvas, 50¹/₄×38
Collection Reader's Digest,
Pleasantville, New York

115 *Homage to the Past*, 1944
Signed l.r.
Oil on canvas, 28¹/₈×29³/₄
Collection Mr and Mrs Ludwig
Neugass, New York

116 *Between Darkness and Light*, 1944
Signed l.r.
Oil on canvas, 39³/₈×28³/₄
Private collection, Basle

117 *Christmas*, 1943
Signed l.r.
Pen drawing, India ink on paper

118 *Bonjour Paris*, 1939–42
Signed l.r.
Oil and pastel on cardboard,
24³/₈×18¹/₈
Private collection, Paris

119 *The Falling Angel*, 1923–33–47
Signed l.r.
Oil on canvas, 57⁷/₈×104³/₈
On loan Kunstmuseum, Basle

120 *Midsummer Night's Dream*, 1939
Signed l.l.
Oil on canvas, 46¹/₈×34⁷/₈
Musée de Peinture et de Sculp-
ture, Grenoble

121 *The Green Eye*, 1944
Signed l.r.
Oil on canvas, 22⁷/₈×20¹/₈
Private collection, Paris

122 *War*, 1943
Signed l.c.r.
Oil on canvas, 41³/₈×29⁷/₈
Musée National d'Art Moderne,
Paris

123 *Time is a River without Banks*,
1939
Signed l.l.
Oil on canvas, 40 1/2 × 32 5/8
Museum of Modern Art, New
York

124 *Vase of Flowers, At Night*, 1943
Signed l.l.
Oil on canvas, 34 1/4 × 24 1/4
Collection Mrs Leo M. Glass,
New York

125 *Wedding*, 1944
Signed l.c.
Oil on canvas, 37 1/2 × 29 1/4
Private collection, Basle

126 *Horse and Child*, 1944
Unsigned
Oil on canvas, 13 2/3 × 22
Private collection, Chicago

127 *The Sleeping Guitar*, 1943
Signed l.r.
Gouache on paper, 25 1/4 × 19 1/4
Private collection, Zurich

128 *Listening to the Cock*, 1944
Signed l.r.
Oil on canvas, 39 × 28 1/8
Collection A. A. Juviler, New
York

129 *Autumn Village*, 1939–45
Signed l.r.
Oil on canvas
Wadsworth Athenaeum, Hart-
ford, Connecticut

130 *Obsession*, 1943
Signed l.r.
Oil on canvas, 30 1/4 × 42 1/2
Private collection, France

131 *The Flying Sleigh*, 1945
Signed l.l.
Oil on canvas, 51 1/8 × 27 5/8
The Abrams Family Collection,
New York

132 *Self-portrait*, 1947
Signed l.r.
Oil on canvas, 27 5/8 × 19 5/8
Collection Mr and Mrs Bernard
J. Reis, New York

133 *Nocturne*, 1947
Signed l.l.
Oil on canvas, 35 3/8 × 28 3/4
Private collection

134 *Green Night*, 1948
Signed l.r.
Gouache and pastel on paper,
18 1/4 × 18 7/8
Collection Maurice Jardot, Paris

135 *The Blue Violinist*, 1947
Signed l.l.
Oil on canvas, 32 1/4 × 24 3/4
Collection Mrs James McLane,
Los Angeles

136 *Winter Sky*, 1942–50
Signed l.r.
Oil on canvas, 33 1/2 × 22 1/2
Collection Mrs Elizabeth H.
Rübel, Connecticut

137 *The Black Glove*, 1948
Signed l.l.
Oil on canvas, 43 5/8 × 32
Private collection, Paris

138 Brush drawing, India ink
From *Four Tales from the Arabian
Nights* portfolio
New York: Pantheon Books,
1948

139 *Fishes at Saint-Jean*, 1949
Signed l.l.
Gouache on paper, $31^{1}/_{8} \times 22^{7}/_{8}$
Collection Dr Nacht, Paris

140 *The Sofa*, 1950
Signed l.r.
Gouache and pastel on paper
Collection Ida Meyer-Chagall,
Basle

141 *Mauve Nude with Two Heads*,
1950
Signed l.r.
Gouache and wash-tint on paper
Collection Ida Meyer-Chagall,
Basle

142 *The Goat*
Unsigned
Pen drawing, India ink on card-
board, $3^{7}/_{8} \times 5^{7}/_{8}$
Private collection, Basle

143 *Blue Circus*, 1950
Signed l.r.
Oil on canvas, $91^{3}/_{8} \times 68^{7}/_{8}$
Artist's collection

144 *Vence: Night*, 1952–6
Signed l.l.
Oil on canvas, $38^{1}/_{8} \times 51$
Private collection, Zurich

145 *Bouquet at Saint-Jean*, 1949
Signed l.r.
Gouache on paper
Collection M. Tériade, Paris

146 Red dish
Signed on the outside
Ceramic, diameter: $13^{3}/_{4}$
Artist's collection

147 Black pitcher
Signed on the bottom
Ceramic, height: 15
Artist's collection

148 *Boy and Dervish*
Lithograph, illustration for *Ara-
bian Nights*
O'Hana Gallery, London

149 *Green Landscape*, 1949
Signed l.r.
Gouache and pastel on paper,
$29^{7}/_{8} \times 21^{5}/_{8}$
Private collection, Switzerland

150 *Quai de la Tournelle*, 1953
Signed l.r.
Oil on canvas
Collection M. A. Goldstein,
Milan

151 *Portrait of Vava*, 1953–6
Signed l.l.
Oil on canvas, $37^{3}/_{8} \times 28^{3}/_{4}$
Collection Vava Chagall, Vence

152 *The Panthéon*, 1953
Signed l.r.
Oil on canvas, $28^{3}/_{8} \times 36^{1}/_{4}$
Collection L.-G. Clayeux, Paris

153 *The Carrousel of the Louvre*,
1953–6
Signed l.l.
Oil on canvas, $37^{5}/_{8} \times 31^{1}/_{2}$
Private collection

154 *Bouquet and Red Circus*, 1960
Unsigned
Oil on canvas, $51^{1}/_{8} \times 77^{5}/_{8}$
Private collection

155 *The Creation of Man*, 1956–8
Signed l.l.
Oil on canvas, $118^1/_2 \times 78^3/_4$
Artist's collection

156 *Sunflowers*, 1955
Signed l.l.
Oil on canvas, $57^7/_8 \times 23^5/_8$
Galerie Maeght, Paris

157 *The Opéra*, 1953
Signed l.l.
Oil on canvas, $36^1/_4 \times 28^2/_3$
Collection Anatole Litvak, Paris

158 *Clown with Violin*, 1956
Signed l.l.
Gouache on paper, $25^5/_8 \times 19^5/_8$
Collection Mr and Mrs N. H.
Sherman, Chicago

159 *The Red Jacket*, 1961
Signed l.r.
Gouache and pastel on paper,
$26 \times 20^1/_8$
Collection Victor Loeb, Berne

160 *Equestrienne*, 1955
Signed l.r.
India ink and gouache on paper,
$41^3/_8 \times 29^1/_2$
Artist's collection

161 *Acrobat*, 1955
Signed l.l.
India ink and gouache on paper
Artist's collection

162 *The Flute Player*, 1954
Signed l.l.
Gouache on paper, $24 \times 18^7/_8$
Private collection, France

163 *The Green Cock*, 1956
Signed l.l.
Oil on canvas, 26×16
Collection Mr and Mrs Henry
A. Markus, Chicago

164 *Boat with Two Fishes*, 1952
Signed l.r.
Gouache and pastel on paper,
$26^3/_8 \times 19^1/_4$
Private collection

165 *The Sun at Poros*, 1952
Signed l.l.
Gouache and pastel on paper,
$26^3/_4 \times 19^1/_4$
Private collection

166–7 Details from the canvas panels
of the Paris Opéra ceiling
Photo Dubout

168 The Paris Opéra ceiling, 1964
Photo Izis

169 *The Tree of Jesse*, 1960
Signed l.l.
Oil on canvas, $59 \times 47^1/_4$
Collection Marcus Diener, Basle

170 *The Three Acrobats*, 1959
Signed l.r.
Oil on canvas, $39^1/_4 \times 24$
Private collection

171 *The Tribe of Benjamin*
Signed l.r.
Stained-glass window for syna-
gogue of Hadassah Clinic, near
Jerusalem
11 ft $1^1/_8$ in $\times$ 8 ft $2^7/_8$ in

172 *Cain and Abel*, 1911
Signed u.r.
Gouache on paper, $8^5/_8 \times 11^1/_8$
Private collection, Basle

173 *Solitude*, 1933
Signed l.r.
Oil on canvas, $40^1/_8 \times 66^1/_3$
Museum, Tel Aviv

174 *The Crucified*, 1944
Signed l.r.
Gouache on paper, $24^1/_2 \times 18^5/_8$
Collection Mr and Mrs Victor
Babin, Cleveland, Ohio

175 *Flayed Ox*, 1947
Signed l.r.
Oil on canvas, $39^3/_4 \times 31^7/_8$
Private collection, Paris

176 *Descent from the Cross*, 1941
Signed l.r.
Gouache on paper, $19^1/_8 \times 13$
Collection Mrs James McLane,
Los Angeles

177 *Synagogue at Safad*, 1931
Signed l.r.
Oil on canvas, $19^5/_8 \times 26$
Stedelijk Museum, Amsterdam

178 *The Wailing Wall*, 1932
Signed l.c.
Oil on canvas, $28^3/_8 \times 36^1/_4$
Private collection, Paris

179 *Elijah's Vision*
Plate 88 of *Bible*
Signed l.c.

Etching and dry point,
$12^1/_2 \times 7^3/_4$

180 *The Purple Angel*, 1941
Signed l.r.
Gouache on paper
Collection Mr and Mrs W.
Paepcke, Chicago

181 *The Sacrifice of Abraham*, 1963
Stained-glass window for the
Cathedral of Metz

182 *The Dream of Jacob*, 1963
Stained-glass window for the
Cathedral of Metz

183 *Blue Crucifixion*, 1941
Signed l.r.
Gouache on paper, $21^7/_8 \times 14^7/_8$
Collection Mrs James McLane,
Los Angeles

184 *Resurrection at the River*, 1947
Signed l.r.
Oil on canvas, $29^1/_8 \times 39$
Private collection

185 *Jacob Wrestling with the Angel*,
1955
Signed l.r.
India ink and gouache on paper
Artist's collection

186 *Offerings*, 1959
Signed l.r.
Gouache and pastel on paper,
$14^7/_8 \times 22$
Collection Mr and Mrs Monroe
Geller, New York

Index

Numbers in italics indicate plates

Aleichem, Shalom, 43; *Miniatures*, illustrations for, 89, *59*
Aleko (ballet), 196
Alice in Wonderland, Lewis Carrol, 155
Apollinaire, Guillaume, 103–6, 110, 112, 114, 115, 127
Arabian Nights, The, 216

Baudelaire, Charles, 91
Bible illustrations, 156, 166, 174, 210, 248, 250–51, *179*, 253–4
Bonnard, Pierre, 208
Brodsky, Valentine, *see* Chagall, Vava

Canudo, Riciotto, 114
Cassirer, Paul, 130
Chagall, Bella (the artist's first wife), 39, 54, 69, 72, 139–48
Chagall, Feiga-Ita (the artist's mother), 21
Chagall (grandfather), 44, 46–7, 68
Chagall, Ida (the artist's daughter), 69
Chagall, Vava (the artist's second wife), 218–9, 231
Chaplin, Charlie, 152–3
Cendrars, Blaise, 22, 54, 114, 115
Ceramics, 215, 216
Cirque Vollard, 148
Courbet, Gustave, 112
Cubism, 100–108, 112, 115, 242

Daphnis and Chloe, illustrations for, 210, 231, 235
Dead Man, The, 7, 20, 21, 43–6, 95–6, 100
Dead Souls, Gogol, illustrations for, *60*, 92, *79*, 130, 132–3, 210

Dedicated to my Fiancée, *9*, 22
Delaunay, Robert, 105–6, 108; and Sonia, 163
Delteil, Joseph, 163
Dizengoff, Meier, 248
Dubnov, Simon, 174
Dürer, Albrecht, 116

Efross, Abraham, 62
El Greco, 193
Eluard, Paul, 128
Engraving, 129–30, 156, 250–1
Ernst, Max, 126
Expressionism, 126

Fables, La Fontaine, illustrations for, 139, 148–9, *90*, 151, 155, 156, *95*, 159, 210
Fauvism, 100–101
Firebird, curtain, scenery, costumes, 212
First Meeting, 146, 148
Fort, Louis, 156
Futurism, 108, 125

Gleizes, Albert, 108
Gogol, Nikolai V., 92, 131–3; see also *The Inspector General* and *Dead Souls*
Granowsky, Alexis, 87–9

Hegel, 252, 253
Holy Carter, The, *11*, 22

I and the Village, *12*, 24, 34, 43, 108
Inspector General, The, Gogol, stage settings for, *61*, 92, 131
Impressionism, 122

Jacob, Max, 114

Jerusalem windows, *171*, 240, 258, 260, 263

Kamerny Jewish State Theatre, 87

La Fontaine, see *Fables*
Léger, Fernand, 108
Lenin, Vladimir Ilich, 172
Leymarie, Jean, 263
Lhote, André, 174
Lipchitz, Jacques, 161
Lithography, 130, 216, 218
Lunacharsky, A. V., 77

Maeght, Aimé, *Derrière le Miroir*, 218
Marq, Charles and Brigitte, 254
Maillol, Aristide, 163
Mallarmé, Stephen, 54
Maritain, Jacques and Raïssa, 163
Massine, Leonide, 196
Metz windows, 254, 256–8, *181–2*
Metzinger, Jean, 108
Meyer, Franz, 45, 76, 106, 155, 204, 247
Meyerhold, V. E., 88
Monet, Claude, 122
Mourlot, Fernand, 218
My Life, by Marc Chagall, 20, 39

Nietzsche, quoted 15
Neuch (the artist's uncle), 44, 51–2

Opéra ceiling, *166–8*, 235, 264
Orphism, 106

'Paris series', 204, 220–29
Pèn, Jehuda, 21, 62
Peretz, Isaac Loeb, 43
Pissanewsky, 21
Playboy of the Western World, Synge, illustrations for, 88, *80*, 132
Potin, Maurice, 156

Pushkin, Alexander S., 196

Razume, 92
Rembrandt, 251
Renoir, Auguste, 208
Repin, Ilya E., 21
Rotermund, H. M., 260
Russian Village, from the Moon, 10, 22

Salmon, André, 114
Schiffrin, Jacques, 216
Schneider, Daniel E., *A Psychoanalytic Approach to the Painting of Marc Chagall*, 28
Schwitters, Kurt, 126
Shakespeare, William, 153, 155
Stanislavsky, Konstantin, 88, 89
Struck, Herman, 129, 248
Suprematists, 86
Surrealism, 127, 128
Sweeny, James Johnson, 26, 45, 194
Synge, see *Playboy of the Western World*

Tairoff, Alexander, 88
Tchaikovsky, Piotr Ilich, 196
Tériade, E., 208, 210, 218, 250
Thousand and One Nights, illustrations for, 216
Time is a River without Banks, 54, *123*, 155
Tintoretto, 254
To Russia, Asses and Others, 15, 24, 28–30, 43
Tugendhold, Jakob A., 62

Van Gogh, Vincent, 100
Venturi, Lionello, 45
Vollard, Ambroise, 139, 148–9, 248, 250

Walden, Herwarth, 126, 242
Watchtangoff, Evgeni, 89
White Crucifixion, 166, 112, 242–3